D0340683

The
Divine Conquest

The Divine Conquest

by

A. W. TOZER

Introduction by
William L. Culbertson

CHRISTIAN PUBLICATIONS, INC.

Harrisburg, Pa.

New York (10): 158 Fifth Avenue
London (E.C.4): 29 Ludgate Hill
Glasgow (C.2): 229 Bothwell Street

TO

*all those Pilgrims of Eternity
whose distrust with earth
has constrained them
to seek in God a more enduring substance,
this little work is offered
in humble dedication.*

Contents

Introduction

THIS BOOK CONTAINS strong medicine, bitter to the taste but potent if taken in contrition and in belief. For a generation content in its own smugness, emotionally exhausted by the claptrap and bunkum of some well-meaning but misled leaders, glibly familiar with all the niceties of careful theological phrases, the medicine may be too bitter. Only the hopeless will benefit. May the slain of the Lord be many; may the hopeless be multiplied. Only then can we experience what some of us know by rote.

Some will point out where they disagree. Too much this or too much that, will be the dodge. Don't be among them. What if something is said differently? What if the preacher holds another view of sovereignty, of holiness, of man (he may be right)? Don't miss the pith because you are engrossed in a study of the bark.

The author is a prophet, a man of God; his life as well as his sermons attest that fact. Here he speaks; no, he preaches; no, he thunders the message of God for those of us who are dreadfully poverty-stricken, though we think we are rich and have need of nothing. Don't be afraid of the thunderings of the language. Don't even fear the bold, jagged strokes of the lightning of the speech. For all who will hear, for all who will obey, here is God's answer to our need—Himself.

WILLIAM CULBERTSON,
PRESIDENT, MOODY BIBLE INSTITUTE.

Preface

It is, I suppose, quite impossible for anyone familiar with the Old Testament to sit down to the writing of a book without remembering with some uneasiness the words of the preacher, the son of David, king in Jerusalem, "And further, by these, my son, be admonished: of making many books there is no end; and much study is a weariness of the flesh."

I think we may safely conclude that the world has by that tired utterance been spared the ordeal of a vast number of worthless books which might otherwise have gotten themselves written. For this we may be indebted to the wise old king more deeply than we know. But if the remembrance of the many books already written has helped even a little to check the making of other poor ones may it not also have worked to prevent the appearance of some which might indeed have held an authentic message for mankind? I do not think so.

The only book that should ever be written is one that flows up from the heart, forced out by the inward pressure. When such a work has gestated within a man it is almost certain that it will be written. The man who is thus charged with a message will not be turned back by any blasé considerations. His book will be to him not only imperative, it will be inevitable.

This little book of the spiritual way has not been "made" in any mechanical sense; it has been born out of inward necessity. At the risk of getting myself into doubtful company I might claim for myself the testimony of Elihu, the son of Barachel the Buzite, of the kindred of Ram, "For I am full of matter, the spirit within me constraineth me." And his fear that if he did not speak he must as a new bottle "burst asunder" is well understood by me. The sight of the languishing church around me and the operations of a new spiritual power within me have set up a pressure impossible to resist. Whether or not the book ever reaches a wide public, still it has to be written if for no other reason than to relieve an unbearable burden on the heart.

Along with this frank account of its spiritual genesis let me further say (and waive the seeming contradiction) that I claim for the book neither originality nor any degree of inspiration beyond that which may be enjoyed by any of the servants of Christ. The "pressure" of which I speak may prove to be nothing more than the squeeze and stress which result from the effort to be good in a bad world and to honor God in the midst of a generation of Christians which seems bent upon giving glory to everyone else but Him.

As for originality, has not someone remarked that no one since Adam has been wholly original? "Every man," said Emerson, "is a quotation from his ancestors." All that I can hope is that this book may

be a right emphasis coming at a right time. If the
reader should discover here anything really new he
is in conscience bound to reject it, for whatever in
religion is new is by the same token false.

Without a doubt the reader will detect upon
these pages traces of other hearts beside my own. I
would be the first to point out that the influence of
many minds is everywhere upon them. The masters
of the inner life are here (however imperfectly repre-
sented), the saintly teachers at whose feet I have sat
long and lovingly and from whose wells I have drawn
water with reverence and gratitude. I lift thankful
eyes to God for the men who have taught me to desire
the better way: Nicholas Herman and that other
Nicholas of Cusa and Meister Eckhart and Fenelon
and Faber. These I name because they have helped
me most, but there have been many others also,
among them being quaint old "John Smith, M.A.,"
whose name renders him almost anonymous, and
about whom I know nothing except that his style
is like that of Lord Francis Bacon and his spirit like
the spirit of the Fourth Gospel and that he once
thoughtfully published a few of his sermons, one of
which, in a happy moment, a veteran missionary
kindly placed in my hands.

Toward anything like thorough scholarship I
make no claim. I am not an authority on any man's
teaching; I have never tried to be. I take my help
where I find it and set my heart to graze where the
pastures are greenest. Only one stipulation do I
make: my teacher must know God, as Carlyle said,
"otherwise than by hearsay," and Christ must be all

in all to him. If a man have only correct doctrine to offer me I am sure to slip out at the first intermission to seek the company of someone who has seen for himself how lovely is the face of Him who is the Rose of Sharon and the Lily of the Valleys. Such a man can help me, and no one else can.

The argument of this book is the *essential interiority* of true religion. I expect to show that if we would know the power of the Christian message our nature must be invaded by an Object from beyond it; that That which is external must become internal; that the objective Reality which is God must cross the threshold of our personality and take residence within.

In arguing thus it could be said that I am wrong, but as Blake once wrote, "If I am wrong, I am wrong in good company." For is it not simply another way of saying, "It is the Spirit that giveth life; the flesh profiteth nothing"? The essentiality of a right interior life was the burden of Christ's teaching, and was without doubt one of the main causes of His rejection by those notorious externalists, the Pharisees. Paul also preached continually the doctrine of the indwelling Christ, and history will reveal that the Church has gained or lost power exactly as she has moved toward or away from the inwardness of her faith.

Perhaps a word of warning would not be amiss here: It is that we beware the common habit of putting confidence in books, as such. It takes a determined effort of the mind to break free from the error of making books and teachers ends in themselves.

The worst thing a book can do for a Christian is to leave him with the impression that he has received from it anything really good; the best it can do is to point the way to the Good he is seeking. The function of a good book is to stand like a signpost directing the reader toward the Truth and the Life. That book serves best which early makes itself unnecessary, just as a signpost serves best after it is forgotten, after the traveler has arrived safely at his desired haven. The work of a good book is to incite the reader to moral action, to turn his eyes toward God and urge him forward. Beyond that it cannot go.

Something should be said here also about the word *religion* as it occurs throughout these pages. I know how carelessly the word has been used by many and how many definitions it has received at the hands of philosophers and psychologists. In order that I may be as clear as possible let me state that the word *religion* as I use it here means the total of God's work in a man and the total of the man's response to that inner working. I mean the power of God at work in the soul as the individual knows and experiences it. But the word has other denotations as well. Sometimes it will mean doctrine, again it will mean the Christian faith or Christianity in its broadest sense. It is a good word and a scriptural one. I shall try to use it carefully, but I invoke the reader's charity to forgive the fault should he encounter it more frequently than he would wish.

It is impossible to travel south without turning one's back upon the north. One cannot plant until he has plowed nor move forward until he has removed the obstacles before him. It is quite to be expected therefore that a bit of gentle criticism should be found here occasionally. Whatever stands in the way of spiritual progress I have felt it my duty to oppose, and it is hardly possible to oppose without injuring the feelings of some. The dearer the error, the more dangerous and the more difficult to correct, always.

But I would bring everything to the test of the Word and the Spirit. Not the Word only, but the Word and the Spirit. "God is a spirit," said our Lord, "and they that worship him must worship him in spirit and in truth." While it is never possible to have the Spirit without at least some measure of truth, it is, unfortunately, possible to have the shell of truth without the Spirit. Our hope is that we may have both the Spirit and the truth in fullest measure.

The
Divine Conquest

I

The Eternal Continuum

AS I WAS WITH MOSES,
SO I WILL BE WITH THEE.
Joshua 1:5

THE UNCONDITIONED PRIORITY of God in His universe
is a truth celebrated both in the Old Testament and
in the New. The prophet Habakkuk sang it in
ecstatic language, "Art thou not from everlasting,
O Lord, my God, mine Holy One?" The apostle
John set it forth in careful words deep with meaning,
"In the beginning was the Word, and the Word was
with God, and the Word was God. The same was in
the beginning with God. All things were made by
him; and without him was not any thing made that
was made."

This truth is so necessary to right thoughts about
God and ourselves that it can hardly be too strongly
emphasized. It is a truth known to everyone, a kind
of common property of all religious persons, but for
the very reason that it is so common it now has but
little meaning for any of us. It has suffered the fate
of which Coleridge writes, "Truths, of all others the
most awful and interesting, are too often considered

as *so* true, that they lose all the power of truth, and lie bed-ridden in the dormitory of the soul, side by side with the most despised and exploded errors." The Divine Priority is one of those "bed-ridden" truths. I desire to do what I can to rescue it "from the neglect caused by the very circumstance of its universal admission." Neglected Christian truths can be revitalized only when by prayer and long meditation we isolate them from the mass of hazy ideas with which our minds are filled and hold them steadily and determinedly in the focus of the mind's attention.

For all things God is the great Antecedent. Because He is, we are and everything else is. He is that "dread, unbeginning One," self-caused, self-contained and self-sufficient. Faber saw this when he wrote his great hymn in celebration of God's eternity.

> *Thou hast no youth, great God,*
> *An Unbeginning End Thou art;*
> *Thy glory in itself abode,*
> *And still abides in its own tranquil heart:*
> *No age can heap its outward years on Thee:*
> *Dear God! Thou art Thyself Thine own eternity.*

Do not skip this as merely another poem. The difference between a great Christian life and any other kind lies in the quality of our religious concepts, and the ideas expressed in these six lines *can* be like rungs on Jacob's ladder leading upward to a sounder and more satisfying idea of God.

We cannot think rightly of God until we begin to think of Him as always being *there,* and *there first.*

Joshua had this to learn. He had been so long the servant of God's servant Moses, and had with such assurance received God's word at his mouth, that Moses and the God of Moses had become blended in his thinking, so blended that he could hardly separate the two thoughts; by association they always appeared together in his mind. Now Moses is dead, and lest the young Joshua be struck down with despair God spoke to assure him, "As I was with Moses, so I will be with thee." Moses was dead, but the God of Moses still lived. Nothing had changed and nothing had been lost. Nothing of God dies when a man of God dies.

"As I was—so I will be." Only God could say this. Only the Eternal One could stand in the timeless I AM and say, "I was" and "I will be."

Here we acknowledge (and there is fear and wonder in the thought) the essential unity of God's nature, the timeless persistence of His changeless Being throughout eternity and time. Here we begin to see and feel the Eternal Continuum. Begin where we will, God is there first. He is Alpha and Omega, the beginning and the ending, which was, and which is, and which is to come, the Almighty. If we grope back to the farthest limits of thought where imagination touches the pre-creation void, we shall find God there. In one unified present glance He comprehends all things from everlasting, and the flutter of a seraph's wing a thousand ages hence is seen by Him now without moving His eyes.

Once I should have considered such thoughts to be mere metaphysical bric-a-brac without practical meaning for anyone in a world such as this. Now I recognize them as sound and easy-to-grasp truths with unlimited potential for good. Failure to get a right viewpoint in the beginning of our Christian lives may result in weakness and sterility for the rest of our days. May not the inadequacy of much of our spiritual experience be traced back to our habit of skipping through the corridors of the Kingdom like children through the market place, chattering about everything, but pausing to learn the true value of nothing?

In my creature impatience I am often caused to wish that there were some way to bring modern Christians into a deeper spiritual life painlessly by short easy lessons; but such wishes are vain. No short cut exists. God has not bowed to our nervous haste nor embraced the methods of our machine age. It is well that we accept the hard truth now: *the man who would know God must give time to Him.* He must count no time wasted which is spent in the cultivation of His acquaintance. He must give himself to meditation and prayer hours on end. So did the saints of old, the glorious company of the apostles, the goodly fellowship of the prophets and the believing members of the holy Church in all generations. And so must we if we would follow in their train.

We would think of God, then, as maintaining the unity of His uncreated Being throughout all His works and His years, as ever saying not only, "I did," and "I will do," but also "I do" and "I am doing." A robust faith requires that we grasp this truth firmly, yet we know how seldom such a thought enters our minds. We habitually stand in our *now* and look back by faith to see the past filled with God. We look forward and see Him inhabiting our future; but our *now* is uninhabited except for ourselves. Thus we are guilty of a kind of pro tem atheism which leaves us alone in the universe while, for the time, God is not. We talk of Him much and loudly, but we secretly think of Him as being absent, and we think of ourselves as inhabiting a parenthetic interval between the God who was and the God who will be. And we are lonely with an ancient and cosmic loneliness. We are each like a little child lost in a crowded market, who has strayed but a few feet from its mother, yet because she cannot be seen the child is inconsolable. So we try by every method devised by religion to relieve our fears and heal our hidden sadness; but with all our efforts we remain unhappy still, with the settled despair of men alone in a vast and deserted universe.

But for all our fears we are not alone. Our trouble is that we *think* of ourselves as being alone. Let us correct the error by thinking of ourselves as standing by the bank of a full flowing river; then let us think of that river as being none else but God Himself. We glance to our left and see the river coming full out of our past; we look to the right and see it flowing on into our future. *But we see also that it is flowing through our present.* And in our today it is the same as it was in our yesterday, not less than, nor different from, but the very same river, one unbroken continuum, undiminished, active and strong as it moves sovereignly on into our tomorrow.

Wherever faith has been original, wherever it has proved itself to be real, it has invariably had upon it a sense of the *present God*. The holy Scriptures possess in marked degree this feeling of actual encounter with a real Person. The men and women of the Bible talked with God. They spoke to Him and heard Him speak in words they could understand. With Him they held person to person converse, and a sense of shining reality is upon their words and deeds.

The world's own prophets, the unbelieving psychologists (those eyeless seekers who seek for a light which is not God's light) have been forced to recognize at the bottom of religious experience this sense of *something there*. But better far is the sense of *Someone there*. It was this that filled with abiding wonder the first members of the Church of Christ. The solemn delight which those early disciples knew sprang straight from the conviction that there was One in the midst of them. They knew that the Majesty in the heavens was confronting them on earth: they were in the very Presence of God. And the power of that conviction to arrest attention and hold it for a lifetime, to elevate, to transform, to fill with uncontrollable moral happiness, to send men singing to prison and to death, has been one of the wonders of history and a marvel of the world.

Our fathers have told us and our own hearts confirm how wonderful is this sense of Someone there. It makes religion invulnerable to critical attack. It secures the mind against collapse under the battering of the enemy. They who worship the God who is present may ignore the objections of unbelieving men. Their experience is self-verifying and needs neither defense nor proof. What they see and hear overwhelms their doubts and confirms their assurance beyond the power of argument to destroy.

Some who desire to be teachers of the Word, but who understand neither what they say, nor whereof they affirm, insist upon "naked" faith as the only way to know spiritual things. By this they mean a conviction of the trustworthiness of the Word of God (a conviction, it may be noted, which the devils share with them). But the man who has been taught even slightly by the Spirit of Truth will rebel at this perversion. His language will be, "I have heard Him and observed Him. What have I to do any more with idols?" For he cannot love a God who is no more than a deduction from a text. He will crave to know God with a vital awareness that goes beyond words, and to live in the intimacy of personal communion. "To seek our divinity merely in books and writings is *to seek the living among the dead;* we do but in vain many times seek God in these, where His truth too often is not so much enshrined as entombed. He is best discerned by an intellectual touch of Him. We must see with our eyes, and hear with our ears, and our hands must handle of the word of life." Nothing can take the place of the *touch* of God in the soul and the sense of Someone there. Real faith, indeed, brings such realization, for real faith is never the operation of reason upon texts. Where true faith is, the knowledge of God will be given as a fact of consciousness altogether apart from the conclusions of logic.

Were a man to awaken in the pitch dark at midnight and hear someone moving about in his room, and know that the unseen presence was a loved member of his family who had every right to be there, his heart might be filled with a sense of quiet pleasure; but should he have reason to believe that an intruder had entered, perhaps to rob or to kill, he would lie in terror and stare at the darkness not knowing from which direction the expected blow might come. But *the difference between experience and no experience would be that acute sense of someone there.* Is it not true that for most of us who call ourselves Christians there is no real experience? We have substituted theological ideas for an arresting encounter; we are full of religious notions, but our great weakness is that for our hearts there is no one there.

Whatever else it embraces, true Christian experience must always include a genuine encounter with God. Without this, religion is but a shadow, a reflection of reality, a cheap copy of an original once enjoyed by someone else of whom we have heard. It cannot but be a major tragedy in the life of any man to live in a church from childhood to old age and know nothing more real than some synthetic god compounded of theology and logic, but having no eyes to see, no ears to hear, and no heart to love.

The spiritual giants of old were men who at

some time became acutely conscious of the real Presence of God and maintained that consciousness for the rest of their lives. The first encounter may have been one of terror, as when a "horror of great darkness" fell upon Abram, or as when Moses at the bush hid his face because he was afraid to look upon God. Usually this fear soon lost its content of terror and changed after a while to delightsome awe, to level off finally into a reverent sense of complete nearness to God. The essential point is, *they experienced God.* How otherwise can the saints and prophets be explained? How otherwise can we account for the amazing power for good they have exercised over countless generations? Is it not that they walked in conscious communion with the real Presence and addressed their prayers to God with the artless conviction that they were addressing Someone actually there?

Without doubt we have suffered the loss of many spiritual treasures because we have let slip the simple truth that the miracle of the perpetuation of life is in God. God did not create life and toss it from Him like some petulant artist disappointed with his work. All life is in Him and out of Him, flowing from Him and returning to Him again, a moving indivisible sea of which He is the Fountainhead. That eternal life which was with the Father is now the possession of believing men, and that life is not God's gift only, but His very Self.

Redemption is not a strange work which God for a moment turned aside to do; rather it is His same work performed in a new field, the field of human catastrophe. The regeneration of a believing soul is but a recapitulation of all His work done from the moment of creation. It is hard to miss the parallel between generation as described in the Old Testament and regeneration as described in the New. How, for instance, could the condition of a lost soul better be described than by the words, "without form and void," with darkness "upon the face of the deep"? And how could the strong yearnings of God's heart over that lost soul be more perfectly expressed than by saying that "the Spirit of God brooded upon the face of the waters"? And from what source could light come to that sin-shrouded soul had God not said, "Let there be light"? At His word the light breaks and the lost man arises to drink of eternal life and follow the Light of the World. As order and fruitfulness came next to that ancient creation, so moral order and spiritual fruit follow next in human experience. And we know that God is the same and His years fail not. He will always act like Himself wherever He is found at work and whatever work He is doing.

We need to seek deliverance from our vain and weakening wish to go back and recover the past. We should seek to be cleansed from the childish notion that to have lived in Abram's day, or in Paul's, would have been better than to live today. With God Abram's day and this day are the same. By one single impulse of life He created all days and all times, so that the life of the first day and the life of the remotest future day are united in Him. We may

well sing again (and believe) the truth our fathers
sang:

> *Eternity with all its years,*
> *Stands present in thy view;*
> *To Thee there's nothing old appears;*
> *Great God, there's nothing new.*

In saving men God is but doing again (or rather con-
tinuing to do) the same creative work as at the beginning of the world. To Him each ransomed soul
is a world wherein He performs again His pleasant
work as of old.

We who experience God in this day may rejoice
that we have in Him all that Abraham or David or
Paul could have; indeed the very angels before the
throne can have no more than we, for they can have
no more than God and can want nothing apart from
Him. And all that He is and all that He has done is
for us and for all who share the common salvation.
With full consciousness of our own demerit we may
yet take our place in the love of God, and the poorest
and weakest of us may without offense claim for ourselves all the riches of the Godhead in mercy given.
I have every right to claim all for myself, knowing
that an infinite God can give all of Himself to each of
His children. He does not distribute Himself that
each may have a part, but to each one He gives all
of Himself as fully as if there were no others.

What a difference it makes when we cease being
general (a dodge, incidentally, for pseudo-humility
and unbelief) and become pointed and personal in
our approach to God. Then we shall not fear the
personal pronoun, but shall with all the friends of

God relate it to the One who gave it and claim each one for himself the Person and work of the Triune God. Then we shall see that all that God did was for each of us. Then we can sing: For me Thou didst cover Thyself with light as with a garment and stretch out the heavens like a curtain and lay the foundations of the earth. For me Thou didst appoint the moon for seasons and the sun knoweth his going down. For me Thou didst make every beast of the earth after his kind and every herb bearing seed and every tree in which is the fruit of a tree. For me prophet wrote and psalmist sang. For me holy men spake as they were moved by the Holy Ghost. For me Christ died, and the redemptive benefits of that death are by the miracle of His present life perpetuated forever, as efficacious now as on the day He bowed His head and gave up the ghost. And when He arose the third day it was for me; and when He poured out upon the disciples the promised Holy Spirit it was that He might continue *in me* the work He had been doing *for me* since the morning of the creation.

II

In Word, or in Power

FOR OUR GOSPEL CAME NOT UNTO YOU IN WORD ONLY,
BUT ALSO IN POWER, AND IN THE HOLY GHOST.

1 Thessalonians 1:5

IF ANY MAN BE IN CHRIST, HE IS A NEW CREATURE.

2 Corinthians 5:17

THOU HAST A NAME THAT THOU LIVEST, AND ART DEAD.

Revelation 3:1

To ONE WHO is a student merely, these verses might
be interesting, but to a serious man intent upon gain-
ing eternal life they might well prove more than a
little disturbing. For they evidently teach that the
message of the gospel may be received in either of
two ways: in word only, without power, or in word
with power. Yet it is the same message whether it
comes in word or in power. And these verses teach
also that when the message is received in power it
effects a change so radical as to be called a new creation. But the message may be received without
power, and apparently some have so received it, for
they have a name to live, and are dead. All this is
present in these texts.

By observing the ways of men at play I have
been able to undersand better the ways of men at

prayer. Most men, indeed, play at religion as they play at games, religion itself being of all games the one most universally played. The various sports have their rules and their balls and their players; the game excites interest, gives pleasure and consumes time, and when it is over the competing teams laugh and leave the field. It is common to see a player leave one team and join another and a few days later play against his old mates with as great zest as he formerly displayed when playing *for* them. The whole thing is arbitrary. It consists in solving artificial problems and attacking difficulties which have been deliberately created for the sake of the game. It has no moral roots and is not supposed to have. No one is the better for his self-imposed toil. It is all but a pleasant activity which changes nothing and settles nothing at last.

If the conditions we describe were confined to the ball park we might pass it over without further thought, but what are we to say when this same spirit enters the sanctuary and decides the attitude of men toward God and religion? For the Church has also its fields and its rules and its equipment for playing the game of pious words. It has its devotees, both laymen and professionals, who support the game with their money and encourage it with their presence, but who are no different in life or character from many who take in religion no interest at all.

As an athlete uses a ball so do many of us use words: words spoken and words sung, words written and words uttered in prayer. We throw them swiftly across the field; we learn to handle them with dexterity and grace; we build reputations upon our word-skill and gain as our reward the applause of those who have enjoyed the game. But the emptiness of it is apparent from the fact that after the pleasant religious game *no one is basically any different from what he had been before*. The bases of life remain unchanged, the same old principles govern, the same old Adam rules.

I have not said that religion without power makes no changes in a man's life, only that it makes no fundamental difference. Water may change from liquid to vapor, from vapor to snow and back to liquid again, and still be fundamentally the same. So powerless religion may put a man through many surface changes and leave him exactly what he was before. Right there is where the snare lies. *The changes are in form only, they are not in kind*. Behind the activities of the non-religious man and the man who has received the gospel without power lie the very same motives. An unblessed ego lies at the bottom of both lives, the difference being that the religious man has learned better to disguise his vice. His sins are refined and less offensive than before he took up religion, but the man himself is not a better man in the sight of God. He may indeed be a worse one, for always God hates artificiality and pretense. Selfishness still throbs like an engine at the center of the man's life. True he may learn to "redirect" his selfish impulses, but his woe is that self still lives unrebuked and even unsuspected within his deep heart. He is a victim of religion without power.

The man who has received the Word without

power has trimmed his hedge, but it is a thorn hedge still and can never bring forth the fruits of the new life. Men do not gather grapes of thorns nor figs of thistles. Yet such a man may be a leader in the Church and his influence and his vote may go far to determine what religion shall be in his generation.

The truth received in power shifts the bases of life from Adam to Christ and a new set of motives goes to work within the soul. A new and different Spirit enters the personality and makes the believing man new in every department of his being. His interests shift from things external to things internal, from things on earth to things in heaven. He loses faith in the soundness of external values, he sees clearly the deceptiveness of outward appearances and his love for and confidence in the unseen and eternal world become stronger as his experience widens.

With the ideas here expressed most Christians will agree, but the gulf between theory and practice is so great as to be terrifying. For the gospel is too often preached and accepted without power, and the radical shift which the truth demands is never made. There may be, it is true, a change of some kind; an intellectual and emotional bargain may be struck with the truth, but whatever happens is not enough, not deep enough, not radical enough. The "creature" is changed, but he is not "new." And right there is the tragedy of it. The gospel is concerned with a new life, with a birth upward onto a new level of being, and until it has effected such a re-birth it has not done a saving work within the soul.

Wherever the Word comes without power its

essential content is missed. For there is in divine truth an imperious note, there is about the gospel an urgency, a finality which will not be heard or felt except by the enabling of the Spirit. We must constantly keep in mind that the gospel is not good news only, but a judgment as well upon everyone that hears it. The message of the Cross is good news indeed for the penitent, but to those who "obey not the gospel" it carries an overtone of warning. The Spirit's ministry to the impenitent world is to tell of sin and righteousness and judgment. For sinners who want to cease being wilful sinners and become obedient children of God the gospel message is one of unqualified peace, but it is by its very nature also an arbiter of the future destinies of men.

This secondary aspect is almost wholly overlooked in our day. The *gift* element in the gospel is held to be its exclusive content, and the *shift* element is accordingly ignored. Theological assent is all that is required to make Christians. This assent is called faith, and is thought to be the only difference between the saved and the lost. Faith is thus conceived as a kind of religious magic, bringing to the Lord great delight, and possessing mysterious power to open the kingdom of heaven.

I want to be fair to everyone and to find all the good I can in every man's religious beliefs, but the harmful effects of this faith-as-magic creed are greater than could be imagined by anyone who has not come face to face with them. Large assemblies today are being told fervently that the one essential qualification for heaven is to be an evil man, and the one

sure bar to God's favor is to be a good one. The very
word *righteousness* is spoken only in cold scorn, and
the moral man is looked upon with pity. "A Christian," say these teachers, "is not morally better than a
sinner, the only difference is that he has taken Jesus,
and so he has a Saviour." I trust it may not sound
flippant to inquire, *"A saviour from what?"* If not
from sin and evil conduct and the old fallen life, then
from what? And if the answer is, From the consequences of past sins and from judgment to come, still
we are not satisfied. Is justification from past offenses
all that distinguishes a Christian from a sinner? Can
a man become a believer in Christ and be no better
than he was before? Does the gospel offer no more
than a skilful Advocate to get guilty sinners off free
at the day of judgment?

I think the truth of the matter is not too deep
nor too difficult to discover. Self-righteousness is an
effective bar to God's favor because it throws the sinner back upon his own merits and shuts him out from
the imputed righteousness of Christ. And to be a
sinner confessed and consciously lost *is* necessary to
the act of receiving salvation through our Lord Jesus
Christ. This we joyously admit and constantly assert,
but here is the truth which has been overlooked in
our day, *A sinner cannot enter the kingdom of God.*
The Bible passages which declare this are too many
and too familiar to need repeating here, but the skep-
tical might look at Galatians 5:19-21 and Revelation
21:8. How then can any man be saved? The penitent sinner meets Christ and after that saving encounter he is a sinner no more. The power of the

gospel changes him, shifts the basis of his life from self to Christ, faces him about in a new direction and makes him a new creation. The moral state of the penitent when he comes to Christ does not affect the result, for the work of Christ sweeps away both his good and his evil and turns him into another man. The returning sinner is not saved by some judicial transaction apart from a corresponding moral change. Salvation must include a judicial change of status, but what is overlooked by most teachers is that *it also includes an actual change in the life of the individual.* And by this we mean more than a surface change, we mean a transformation as deep as the roots of his human life. If it does not go that deep it does not go deep enough.

If we had not first suffered a serious decline in our expectations we should not have accepted this tame technical view of faith. The churches (even the gospel churches) are worldly in spirit, morally anemic, on the defensive, imitating instead of initiating and in a wretched state generally because for two full generations they have been told that justification is no more than a "not guilty" verdict pronounced by the Heavenly Father upon a sinner who can present the magic coin *faith* with the wondrous "open-sesame" engraved upon it. If it is not stated as bluntly as that, at least the message is so presented as to create such an impression. The whole business is the result of hearing the Word preached without power and receiving it in the same way.

Now faith is indeed the open-sesame to eternal blessedness. Without faith it is impossible to please

God, neither can any man be saved apart from faith in the risen Saviour. But the true quality of faith is almost universally missed, viz., its moral quality. It is more than mere confidence in the veracity of a statement made in Holy Writ. It is a highly moral thing and of a spiritual essence. It invariably effects radical transformation in the life of the one who exercises it. It shifts the inward gaze from self to God. It introduces its possessor into the life of heaven upon earth.

It is not my desire to minimize the justifying effect of faith. No man who knows the depths of his own wickedness would dare to appear before the ineffable Presence with nothing to recommend him but his own character, nor would any Christian, wise after the discipline of failures and imperfections, want his acceptance with God to depend upon any degree of holiness to which he might have attained through the operations of inward grace. All who know their own hearts and the provisions of the gospel will join in the prayer of the man of God:

> *When He shall come with trumpet sound,*
> *O, may I then in Him be found;*
> *Dressed in His righteousness alone,*
> *Faultless to stand before the throne.*

It is a distressing thing that a truth so beautiful should have been so perverted. But perversion is the price we pay for failure to emphasize the moral content of truth; it is the curse that follows rational orthodoxy when it has quenched or rejected the Spirit of Truth.

In asserting that faith in the gospel effects a change of life-motive from self to God I am but stating the sober facts. Every man with moral intelligence must be aware of the curse that afflicts him inwardly; he must be conscious of the thing we call *ego,* by the Bible called *flesh* or *self,* but by whatever name called, a cruel master and a deadly foe. Pharaoh never ruled Israel as tyrannically as this hidden enemy rules the sons and daughters of men. The words of God to Moses concerning Israel in bondage may well describe us all: "I have surely seen the affliction of my people which are in Egypt, and have heard their cry by reason of their taskmasters; for I know their sorrows." And when, as the Nicene Creed so tenderly states, our Lord Jesus Christ, "for us men, and for our salvation came down from heaven, and was incarnate by the Holy Ghost of the Virgin Mary, and was made man, and was crucified also for us under Pontius Pilate, and suffered and was buried, and the third day He arose again according to the Scriptures, and ascended into heaven, and sitteth on the right hand of the Father," what was it all for? That He might pronounce us technically free and leave us in our bondage? Never. Did not God say to Moses, "I am come down to deliver them out of the hand of the Egyptians, and to bring them up out of that land unto a good land and a large, unto a land flowing with milk and honey . . . and thou shalt say unto Pharaoh, Let my people go"? For sin's human captives God never intends anything less than full deliverance. The Christian message rightly understood means this: The God who by the *word* of the gospel *proclaims* men free, by the *power* of the gospel *actually makes them free.* To accept less than this is to know the gospel in word only, without its power.

They to whom the Word comes in power know this deliverance, this inward migration of the soul from slavery to freedom, this release from moral bondage. They know in experience a radical shift in position, a real crossing over, and they stand consciously on another soil under another sky and breathe another air. Their life motives are changed and their inward drives made new.

What are these old drives that once forced obedience at the end of a lash? What but little taskmasters, servants of the great taskmaster, *Self,* who stand before him and do his will? To name them all would require a book in itself, but we would point out one as a type or sample of the rest. It is the desire for social approval. This is not bad in itself and might be perfectly innocent if we were living in a sinless world, but since the race of men has fallen off from God and joined itself to His foes, to be a friend of the world is to be a collaborator with evil and an enemy of God. Still the desire to please men is back of all social acts from the highest civilizations to the lowest levels upon which human life is found. No one can escape it. The outlaw who flouts the rules of society and the philosopher who rises in thought above its common ways may *seem* to have escaped from the snare, but they have in reality merely narrowed the circle of those they desire to please. The outlaw has his pals before whom he seeks to shine; the philosopher his little coterie of superior thinkers whose approval is necessary to his happiness. For both, the motive-root remains uncut. Each draws his peace from the thought that he enjoys the esteem of his fellows, though each will interpret the whole business in his own way.

Every man looks to his fellow men because he has no one else to whom he can look. David could say, "Whom have I in heaven but Thee? and there is none upon earth that I desire beside Thee," but the sons of this world have not God, they have only each other, and they walk holding to each other and looking to one another for assurance like frightened children. But their hope will fail them, for they are like a group of men, none of whom has learned to fly a plane, who suddenly find themselves aloft without a pilot, each looking to the other to bring them safely down. Their desperate but mistaken trust cannot save them from the crash which must certainly follow.

With this desire to please men so deeply implanted within us how can we uproot it and shift our life-drive from pleasing men to pleasing God? Well, no one can do it alone, nor can he do it with the help of others, nor by education nor by training nor by any other method known under the sun. What is required is a reversal of nature (that it is a fallen nature does not make it any the less powerful) and this reversal must be a supernatural act. That act the Spirit performs through the power of the gospel when it is received in living faith. Then He displaces the old with the new. Then He invades the life as sunlight invades a landscape and drives out the old motives as light drives away darkness from the sky.

The way it works in experience is something like this: The believing man is overwhelmed suddenly by a powerful feeling that *only God matters;* soon this works itself out into his mental life and conditions all his judgments and all his values. Now he finds himself free from slavery to man's opinions. A mighty desire to please only God lays hold of him. Soon he learns to love above all else the assurance that he is well pleasing to the Father in heaven. ✓

It is this complete switch in their pleasure-source that has made believing men invincible. So could saints and martyrs stand alone, deserted by every earthly friend, and die for Christ under the universal displeasure of mankind. When, to intimidate him, Athanasius' judges warned him that the whole world was against him, he dared to reply, "Then is Athanasius against the world!" That cry has come down the years and today may remind us that the gospel has power to deliver men from the tyranny of social approval and make them free to do the will of God.

I have singled out this one enemy for consideration, but it is only one, and there are many others. They seem to stand by themselves and have existence apart from each other, but it is only seeming. Actually they are but branches of the same poison vine, growing from the same evil root, and they die together when the root dies. That root is *self,* and the Cross is its only effective destroyer.

The message of the gospel, then, is the message of a new creation in the midst of an old, the message of the invasion of our human nature by the eternal life of God and the displacing of the old by the new. The new life seizes upon the believing man's nature and sets about its benign conquest, a conquest which is not complete until the invading life has taken full possession and a new creation has emerged. And this is an act of God without human aid, for it is a moral miracle and a spiritual resurrection. ✓

III

The Mystery of the Call

CALLED TO BE AN APOSTLE—CALLED TO BE SAINTS.
1 Corinthians 1:1-2

THE LITTLE WORD, *called,* as used here by the apostle
is like a door opening into another world, and when
we enter we shall find ourselves in another world indeed. For the new world into which we pass is the
world of God's sovereign will where the will of man
cannot come, or if it come it is as a dependent and
a servant, never as a lord.

Paul here explains his apostleship: it is by an
effectual call, not by his own wish or will or determination, and this call is a divine thing, free, uninflu-
enced and altogether out of the hands of man. The
response is from man, but the call, never. That is
from God alone.

There are two worlds, set over against each
other, dominated by two wills, the will of man and
the will of God, respectively. The old world of fallen
nature is the world of human will. There man is
king and his will decides events. So far as he is able in
his weakness he decides who and what and when and
where. He fixes values: what is to be esteemed, what
despised, what received and what rejected. His will

runs through everything. "I determined," "I decided," "I decree," "Be it enacted." These words are heard continually springing from the lips of little men. And how they rejoice in their fancied "right of self-determination," and with what comic vanity do they boast of the "sovereign voter." They do not know, or refuse to consider, that they are but for a day, soon to pass away and be no more.

> Time like an ever rolling stream
> Bears all its sons away,
> They fly forgotten as a dream
> Dies at the break of day.
>
> The busy tribes of flesh and blood
> With all their cares and fears,
> Are carried downward like a flood
> And lost in following years.

Yet in their pride men assert their will and claim ownership of the earth. Well, for a time it is true, this is man's world. God is admitted only by man's sufferance. He is treated as visiting royalty in a democratic country. Everyone takes His name upon his lips and (especially at certain seasons) He is feted and celebrated and hymned. But behind all this flattery men hold firmly to their right of self-determination. As long as man is allowed to play host he will honor God with his attention, but always He must remain a guest and never seek to be Lord. Man will have it understood that this is his world; he will make its laws and decide how it shall be run. God is permitted to decide nothing. Man bows to Him, and as he bows, manages with difficulty to conceal the crown upon his own head.

When we enter the Kingdom of God, however, we are in another kind of world. It is altogether other than the old world from which we came; always it is different from and mostly it is contrary to the old. Where the two appear to be alike it is only in appearance, for the first is of the earth earthy, the second is from heaven. "That which is born of the flesh is flesh, and that which is born of the Spirit is spirit." The first will perish; the last abides forever.

Paul was made an apostle by the direct call of God. "No man taketh this honor upon himself." Among men we see that noted artists sometimes appear before royalty and their appearance is called a "command performance." However gifted they may be and however famous, they dare not intrude into the king's presence except by royal call, a call that amounts to an order. That call leaves no place for refusal except at the risk of affront to majesty. And with Paul it was not otherwise. God's call was also His command. Had Paul been running for political office the voters would have determined the outcome. Had he been trying for a place in the literary world his own abilities would have decided that place for him. Had he been competing in the prize ring his own strength and skill would have won or lost for him. But his apostleship was not so determined.

How delightful are God's ways and the goings forth of His will. Not by might nor by power, neither by native ability nor by training are men made apostles, but by God's effectual calling. So it is with every office within the Church. Men are permitted to recognize the call and make public acknowledgment before the congregation, but never are they permitted themselves to make the choice. But where divine ways and the ways of men mix and mingle there is confusion and failure continually. Good men who are yet not called of God may, and often do, take upon them the sacred work of the ministry. Worse still is it when men who belong yet to the old world and have not been renewed by the miracle of regeneration try to carry on God's holy work. How sad is the sight and how tragic the consequences, for the ways of man and the ways of God are forever contrary one to the other.

Is this one of the reasons behind our present state of spiritual weakness? How can the flesh serve the Spirit? or how can men from another tribe than Levi's minister before the altar? How vain to try to serve the new after the ways of the old. From this stems the rank growth of evil methods which characterizes the churches of our day. The bold and self-assertive push forward and the weak ones follow without asking for a proof of their right to lead. The divine call is ignored, and sterility and confusion result.

It is time for us to seek again the leadership of the Holy Ghost. Man's lordship has cost us too much. Man's intrusive will has introduced such a multiplicity of unspiritual ways and unscriptural activities as positively to threaten the life of the Church. These divert annually millions of dollars from the true work of God and waste Christian man-hours in such vast numbers as to be heartbreaking.

There is another and worse evil which springs from this basic failure to grasp the radical difference between the natures of the two worlds. It is the habit of languidly "accepting" salvation as if it were a small matter and one wholly in our hands. Men are exhorted to think things over and "decide" for Christ, and in some places one day each year is set aside as "Decision Day," at which time people are expected to condescend to grant Christ the right to save them, a right which they have obviously refused Him up to that time. Christ is thus made to stand again before men's judgment seat; He is made to wait upon the pleasure of the individual, and after long and humble waiting is either turned away or patronizingly admitted. By a complete misunderstanding of the noble and true doctrine of the freedom of the human will salvation is made to depend perilously upon the will of man instead of upon the will of God.

However deep the mystery, however many the paradoxes involved, it is still true that men become saints not at their own whim but by sovereign calling. Has not God by such words as these taken out of our hands the ultimate choice? "It is the Spirit that quickeneth; the flesh profiteth nothing . . . All that the Father giveth me shall come to me . . . No man can come to me, except the Father which hath sent me draw him . . . No man can come unto me, except it were given him of my Father . . . Thou hast given him power over all flesh, that he should give eternal life to as many as thou hast given him . . .

It pleased God, who separated me from my mother's womb, and called me by his grace, to reveal his Son in me."

God has made us in His likeness, and one mark of that likeness is our free will. We hear God say, "Whosoever will, let him come." We know by bitter experience the woe of an unsurrendered will and the blessedness or terror which may hang upon our human choice. But back of all this and preceding it is the sovereign right of God to call saints and determine human destinies. The master choice is His, the secondary choice is ours. Salvation is from our side a choice, from the divine side it is a seizing upon, an apprehending, a conquest by the Most High God. *Our "accepting" and "willing" are reactions rather than actions.* The right of determination must always remain with God.

God has indeed lent to every man the power to lock his heart and stalk away darkly into his self-chosen night, as He has lent to every man the ability to respond to His overtures of grace, but while the "no" choice may be ours, the "yes" choice is always God's. He is the Author of our faith as He must be its Finisher. Only by grace can we continue to believe; we can persist in willing God's will only as we are seized upon by a benign power that will overcome our natural bent to unbelief.

So keenly do we men enjoy dominion that we like to think that we hold in our own hands the power of life and death. We love to think that hell will be easier to bear from the fact of our having gone there in defiance of some power that sought to

rule us. He knew this well who put into the mouth
of Satan that speech of proud defiance:

> *What though the field be lost?*
> *All is not lost; the unconquerable will,*
> *The study of revenge, immortal hate,*
> *And courage never to submit or yield,*
> *And what is else not to be overcome;*
> *That glory never shall his wrath or might*
> *Extort from us.*

While few would dare thus to voice their secret feelings, there are millions who have imbibed the notion
that they hold in their hands the keys of heaven and
hell. The whole content of modern evangelistic
preaching contributes to this attitude. Man is made
large and God small; Christ is placed in a position
to excite pity rather than respect as He stands meekly,
lantern in hand, outside a vine-covered door.

How deeply do men err who conceive of God as
subject to our human will or as standing respectfully
to wait upon our human pleasure. Though He in
condescending love may seem to place Himself at
our disposal, yet never for the least division of a
moment does He abdicate His throne or void His
right as Lord of man and nature. He is that Majesty
on high. To Him all angels cry aloud, the heavens
and all the powers therein: to Him cherubim and
seraphim continually do cry, "Holy, Holy, Holy,
Lord God of Sabaoth, heaven and earth are full of
the majesty of thy glory." He is the Fear of Isaac
and the Dread of Jacob, and before Him prophet and

patriarch and saint have knelt in breathless awe and adoration.

The gradual disappearance of the idea and feeling of majesty from the Church is a sign and a portent. The revolt of the modern mind has had a heavy price, how heavy is becoming more apparent as the years go by. Our God has now become our servant to wait on our will. "The Lord is my *shepherd*," we say, instead of *"The Lord* is my shepherd," and the difference is as wide as the world.

We need to have restored again the lost idea of sovereignty, not as a doctrine only but as the source of a solemn religious emotion. We need to have taken from our dying hand the shadow scepter with which we fancy we rule the world. We need to feel and know that we are but dust and ashes, and that God is the disposer of the destinies of men. How ashamed we Christians should be that a pagan king should teach us to fear the Majesty on high. For it was the chastened Nebuchadnezzar who said, "I lifted up mine eyes unto heaven and mine understanding returned unto me, and I blessed the most High, and I praised and honored him that liveth forever, whose dominion is an everlasting dominion, and his kingdom is from generation to generation. And all the inhabitants of the earth are reputed as nothing, and he doeth according to his will in the army of heaven, and among the inhabitants of the earth: and none can stay his hand, or say unto him, What doest thou?"

"At the same time," added the humbled king, "my reason returned unto me." This whole passage

is apt to be overlooked, occurring as it does in one of
the less popular books of the Bible, but is it not of
great significance that *humility* and *reason* returned
together? "Now I Nebuchadnezzar praise and extol
and honor the King of heaven, all whose works are
truth, and his ways judgment: and those that walk
in pride he is able to abase." The king's pride was to
him a kind of insanity which drove him at last into
the fields to dwell with the beasts. While he saw
himself large and God small he was insane; sanity
returned only as he began to see God as all and himself as nothing.

Such moral madness as Nebuchadnezzar suffered
is now upon the nations. Men of reputed learning
have long been chanting with Swinburne, "Glory to
man in the highest," and the masses have picked up
the chant. A strange amentia has resulted, marked
by acute self-importance and delusions of moral
grandeur. Men who refuse to worship the true God
now worship themselves with tender devotion. A
return to spiritual sanity waits for repentance and
true humility. God grant that we may soon know
again how small and how sinful we are.

IV

Victory through Defeat

AND HE SAID, THY NAME SHALL BE CALLED NO
MORE JACOB, BUT ISRAEL: FOR AS A PRINCE
HAST THOU POWER WITH GOD AND WITH MEN,
AND HAST PREVAILED.

Genesis 32:28

BUT GOD FORBID THAT I SHOULD GLORY, SAVE
IN THE CROSS OF OUR LORD JESUS CHRIST, BY
WHOM THE WORLD IS CRUCIFIED UNTO ME,
AND I UNTO THE WORLD.

Galatians 6:14

THE EXPERIENCES OF men who walked with God in
olden times agree to teach that the Lord cannot fully
bless a man until He has first conquered him. The
degree of blessing enjoyed by any man will corre-
spond exactly with the completeness of God's victory
over him. This is a badly neglected tenet of the
Christian's creed, not understood by many in this
self-assured age, but it is nevertheless of living importance to us all. This spiritual principle is well
illustrated in the Book of Genesis.

Jacob was the wily old heel-catcher whose very
strength was to him a near-fatal weakness. For two-
thirds of his total life he had carried in his nature

something hard and unconquered. Not his glorious vision in the wilderness nor his long bitter discipline in Haran had broken his harmful strength. He stood at the ford of Jabbok at the time of the going down of the sun, a shrewd, intelligent old master of applied psychology learned the hard way. The picture he presented was not a pretty one. He was a vessel marred in the making. His hope lay in his own defeat. This he did not know at the setting of day, but had learned before the rising of the sun. All night he resisted God until in kindness God touched the hollow of his thigh and won the victory over him. It was only after he had gone down to humiliating defeat that he began to feel the joy of release from his own evil strength, the delight of God's conquest over him. Then he cried aloud for the blessing and refused to let go till it came. It had been a long fight, but for God (and for reasons known only to Him) Jacob had been worth the effort. Now he became another man, the stubborn and self-willed rebel was turned into a meek and dignified friend of God. He had "prevailed" indeed, but through weakness, not through strength.

Only the conquered can know true blessedness. This is sound philosophy, based upon life, and necessary by the constitution of things. We need not accept this truth blindly; the reasons are discoverable, among them being these: We are created beings, and as such are derived, not self-existent. Not to us has it been given to have life in ourselves. For life we are wholly and continually dependent upon God, the Source and Fountain of life. Only by full dependence upon Him are the hidden potentialities of our natures realized. Apart from this we are but half-men, malformed and unbeautiful members of a noble race once made to wear the image of its Creator.

Once in olden times the Lord declared that the end of all flesh had come before Him, and the years have brought no mitigation of that sentence. "They that are in the flesh cannot please God . . . The carnal mind is enmity against God, for it is not subject to the law of God, neither indeed can be . . . To be carnally minded is death." By such words as these has God perpetuated the ancient sentence of condemnation. Whether we admit it or not the stroke of death is upon us, and it will be saving wisdom for us to learn to trust not in ourselves but in Him that raiseth the dead. For how dare we put confidence in anything so fugitive, so fleeting, as human life?

> *The wise man, I affirm, can find no rest*
> *In that which perishes: nor will he lend*
> *His heart to aught which doth on time depend.*

From across four centuries these words have come to us, and in our moments of quiet wisdom we feel and know them to be true. Why then do we put our trust in things that perish and so become the dupes of time and the fools of change? Who has poisoned our cup and turned us into rebels? That old serpent, the devil, he it was who first beguiled us into that rash declaration of independence, a declaration which, in view of the circumstances, is both deeply comic and profoundly tragic. For our enemy must laugh at the incredible vanity that would lead us to match strength with the Almighty: that is the cynical comedy of it all; the tragedy drops with every tear and sorrows beside every grave.

A little acquaintance with our own hearts will force us to acknowledge that there is no hope within us, and the briefest glance around should show us that we need expect no help from without. Nature itself will teach us that (apart from God) we are but orphans of the creation, waifs of the wide spaces, caught helpless amid the whirl of forces too great to comprehend. Onward through this world roars an immense and sightless power leaving in its wake generations, cities, civilizations. The earth, our brief home, offers us at last only a grave. For us there is nothing safe, nothing kind. In the Lord there is mercy, but in the world there is none, for nature and life move on as if unaware of good or evil, of human sorrow or human pain.

It was to save Jacob from deceptive hope that God confronted him that night on the bank of the river. To save him from self-trust it was necessary for God to conquer him, to wrest control away from him, to take His great power and rule with a rod of love. Charles Wesley, the sweet singer of England, with a spiritual penetration rare even among advanced Christians, wrote from the mouth of Jacob what he conceived to be his prayer as he wrestled with God at the ford of Jabbok:

My strength is gone, my nature dies;
I sink beneath Thy weighty hand;

Faint to revive, and fall to rise:
I fall, and yet by faith I stand.
I stand, and will not let Thee go,
Till I Thy Name, Thy Nature know.

Lame as I am, I take the prey;
Hell, earth, and sin, with ease o'ercome;
I leap for joy, pursue my way,
And as a bounding hart fly home,
Through all eternity to prove,
Thy Nature and Thy Name is love.

We might well pray for God to invade and conquer us, for until He does, we remain in peril from a thousand foes. We bear within us the seeds of our own disintegration. Our moral imprudence puts us always in danger of accidental or reckless self-destruction. The strength of our flesh is an ever present danger to our souls. Deliverance can come to us only by the defeat of our old life. Safety and peace come only after we have been forced to our knees. God rescues us by breaking us, by shattering our strength and wiping out our resistance. Then He invades our natures with that ancient and eternal life which is from the beginning. So He conquers us and by that benign conquest saves us for Himself.

With this open secret awaiting easy discovery, why do we in almost all our busy activities work in another direction from this? Why do we build our churches upon human flesh? Why do we set such store by that which the Lord has long ago repudiated, and despise those things which God holds in such high esteem? For we teach men not to die with

Christ but to live in the strength of their dying man-
hood. We boast not in our weakness but in our
strength. Values which Christ has declared to be
false are brought back into evangelical favor and pro-
moted as the very life and substance of the Christian
way. How eagerly do we seek the approval of this or
that man of worldly reputation. How shamefully do
we exploit the converted celebrity. Anyone will do
to take away the reproach of obscurity from our pub-
licity-hungry leaders: famous athletes, congressmen,
world travelers, rich industrialists; before such we
bow with obsequious smiles and honor them in our
public meetings and in the religious press. Thus we
glorify men to enhance the standing of the Church
of God, and the glory of the Prince of Life is made
to hang upon the transient fame of a man who
shall die.

It is amazing that we can claim to be followers
of Christ and yet take so lightly the words of His
servants. For how could we act as we do if we took
seriously the admonition of James the servant of
God, "My brethren, have not the faith of our Lord
Jesus Christ, the Lord of glory, with respect of persons. For if there come unto your assembly a man
with a gold ring, in goodly apparel, and there come
in also a poor man in vile raiment; And ye have
respect to him that weareth the gay clothing, and say
unto him, Sit thou here in a good place; and say to
the poor, Stand thou there, or sit here under my foot-
stool: Are ye not then partial in yourselves, and are
become judges of evil thoughts? Hearken, my be-
loved brethren, Hath not God chosen the poor of

this world rich in faith, and heirs of the kingdom which he hath promised to them that love him"?

Paul saw these things in another light than did those of whom James makes his complaint. "By the cross," he said, "I am crucified unto the world." The cross where Jesus died became also the cross where His apostle died. The loss, the rejection, the shame, belong both to Christ and to all who in very truth are His. The cross that saves them also slays them, and anything short of this is a pseudo-faith and not true faith at all. But what are we to say when the great majority of our evangelical leaders walk not as crucified men but as those who accept the world at its own value—rejecting only its grosser elements? How can we face Him who was crucified and slain when we see His followers accepted and praised? Yet they preach the cross and protest loudly that they are true believers. Are there then two crosses? And did Paul mean one thing and they another? I fear that it is so, that there are two crosses, the old cross and the new.

Remembering my own deep imperfections I would think and speak with charity of all who take upon them the worthy Name by which we Christians are called. But if I see aright, the cross of popular evangelicalism is not the cross of the New Testament. It is, rather, a new bright ornament upon the bosom of a self-assured and carnal Christianity whose hands are indeed the hands of Abel, but whose voice is the voice of Cain. The old cross slew men; the new cross entertains them. The old cross condemned; the new cross amuses. The old cross destroyed confidence in the flesh; the new cross encourages it. The old cross brought tears and blood; the new cross brings laughter. The flesh, smiling and confident, preaches and sings about the cross; before that cross it bows and toward that cross it points with carefully staged histrionics—but upon that cross it will not die, and the reproach of that cross it stubbornly refuses to bear.

I well know how many smooth arguments can be marshalled in support of the new cross. Does not the new cross win converts and make many followers and so carry the advantage of numerical success? Should we not adjust ourselves to the changing times? Have we not heard the slogan, "New days, new ways"? And who but someone very old and very conservative would insist upon death as the appointed way to life? And who today is interested in a gloomy mysticism that would sentence its flesh to a cross and recommend self-effacing humility as a virtue actually to be practiced by modern Christians? These are the arguments, along with many more flippant still, which are brought forward to give an appearance of wisdom to the hollow and meaningless cross of popular Christianity.

Doubtless there are many whose eyes are open to the tragedy of our times, but why are they so silent when their testimony is so sorely needed? In the name of Christ men have made void the cross of Christ. "The noise of them that sing do I hear." Men have fashioned a golden cross with a graving tool, and before it they sit down to eat and drink and rise up to play. In their blindness they have substituted the work of their own hands for the working of God's power. Perhaps our greatest present need may be the coming of a prophet to dash the stones at the foot of the mountain and call the Church out to repentance or to judgment.

Before all who wish to follow Christ the way lies clear. It is the way of death unto life. Always life stands just beyond death and beckons the man who is sick of himself to come and know the life more abundant. But to reach the new life he must pass through the valley of the shadow of death, and I know that at the sound of those words many will turn back and follow Christ no more. But to whom shall we go? "Thou hast the words of eternal life."

It may be that there are some well disposed followers who draw back because they cannot accept the morbidity which the idea of the cross seems to connote. They are lovers of the sun and find it too hard to think of living always in the shadows. They do not wish to dwell with death nor to live forever in an atmosphere of dying. And their instinct is sound. The Church has made altogether too much of death-bed scenes and churchyards and funerals. The musty smell of churches, the slow and solemn step of the minister, the subdued quiet of the worshippers and the fact that many enter a church only to pay their last respect to the dead all add up to the notion that religion is something to be dreaded, and like a major operation, suffered only because we are caught in a crisis and dare not avoid it. All this is not the religion of the cross; it is rather a gross parody on it. Churchyard Christianity, though not even remotely related to the doctrine of the cross, may yet be partly to blame for the appearance of the new and jolly cross of today. Men crave life, but when they are told that life comes by the cross they cannot understand how it can be, for they have learned to associate with the cross such typical images as memorial placques, dim-lit aisles and ivy. So they reject the true message of the cross and with that message they reject the only hope of life known to the sons of men.

The truth is that God has never planned that His children should live forever stretched upon a cross. Christ Himself endured His cross for only six hours. When the cross had done its work life entered and took over. "Wherefore God also hath highly exalted him, and given him a name which is above every name." His joyful resurrection followed hard upon His joyless crucifixion. But the first had to come before the second. The life that halts short of the cross is but a fugitive and condemned thing, doomed at last to be lost beyond recovery. That life which goes to the cross and loses itself there to rise again with Christ is a divine and deathless treasure. Over it death hath no more dominion. Whoever refuses to bring his old life to the cross is but trying to cheat death, and no matter how hard he may struggle against it, he is nevertheless fated to lose his life at last. The man who takes his cross and follows Christ will soon find that his direction is *away* from the sepulcher. Death is behind him and a joyous and increasing life before. His days will be marked henceforth not by ecclesiastical gloom, the churchyard, the hollow tone, the black robe (which are all but the

cerements of a dead church), but by "joy unspeak·
able and full of glory."

√ Real faith must always mean more than passive
acceptance. It dare mean nothing less than surrender
of our doomed Adam-life to a merciful end upon the
cross. That is, we own God's just sentence against our
evil flesh and admit His right to end its unlovely
career. We reckon ourselves to have been crucified
with Christ and to have risen again to newness of
life. Where such faith is, God will always work in
line with our reckoning. Then begins the divine conquest of our lives. This God accomplishes by an
effective seizing upon, a sharp but love-impelled invasion of our natures. When He has overpowered
our resistance He binds us with the cords of love and
draws us to Himself. There, "faint with His loveliness" we lie conquered and thank God again and
again for the blessed conquest. There, with moral
sanity restored, we lift up our eyes and bless the
Most High God. Then we go forth in faith to appre-
hend that for which we were first apprehended of
God.

"I thank Thee, O Father, Lord of heaven and
earth, because Thou hast hid these things from the
wise and prudent, and hast revealed them unto babes.
Even so, Father, for so it seemed good in thy sight."

V

The Forgotten One

THE COMFORTER, WHICH IS THE HOLY GHOST.
John 14:26

In NEGLECTING OR denying the deity of Christ the Liberals have committed a tragic blunder, for it leaves them nothing but an imperfect Christ whose death was a mere martyrdom and whose resurrection is a myth. They who follow a merely human Saviour follow no Saviour at all, but an ideal only, and one furthermore that can do no more than mock their weaknesses and sins. If Mary's son was not the Son of God in a sense no other man is, then there can be no more hope for the human race. If He who called Himself the Light of the World was only a flickering torch, then the darkness that enshrouds the earth is here to stay. So-called Christian leaders shrug this off, but their responsibility toward the souls of their flocks cannot be dismissed with a shrug. God will yet bring them to account for the injury they have done to the plain people who trusted them as spiritual guides.

But however culpable the act of the Liberal in denying the Godhood of Christ, we who pride ourselves on our orthodoxy must not allow our indignation to blind us to our own shortcomings. Certainly this is no time for self-congratulations, for we too have in recent years committed a costly blunder in religion, a blunder paralleling closely that of the Liberal. Our blunder (or shall we frankly say our sin?) has been to neglect the doctrine of the Spirit to a point where we virtually deny Him His place in the Godhead. This denial has not been by open doctrinal statement, for we have clung closely enough to the Biblical position wherever our credal pronouncements are concerned. Our formal creed is sound; *the breakdown is in our working creed*.

This is not a trifling distinction. A doctrine has practical value only as far as it is *prominent in our thoughts* and *makes a difference in our lives*. By this test the doctrine of the Holy Spirit as held by evangelical Christians today has almost no practical value at all. In most Christian churches the Spirit is quite entirely overlooked. Whether He is present or absent makes no real difference to anyone. Brief reference is made to Him in the Doxology and the Benediction. Further than that He might as well not exist. So completely do we ignore Him that it is only by courtesy that we can be called Trinitarian. The Christian doctrine of the Trinity boldly declares the equality of the Three Persons and the right of the Holy Spirit to be worshipped and glorified. Anything less than this is something less than Trinitarianism.

Our neglect of the doctrine of the blessed Third Person has had and is having serious consequences. For doctrine is dynamite. It must have emphasis sufficiently sharp to detonate it before its power is released. Failing this it may lie quiescent in the back of our minds for the whole of our lives without effect. The doctrine of the Spirit is buried dynamite. Its power awaits discovery and use by the Church. The power of the Spirit will not be given to any mincing assent to pneumatological truth. The Holy Spirit cares not at all whether we write Him into our credenda in the back of our hymnals; He waits for our *emphasis*. When He gets into the thinking of the teachers He will get into the expectation of the hearers. When the Holy Spirit ceases to be incidental and again becomes fundamental the power of the Spirit will be asserted once more among the people called Christians.

The idea of the Spirit held by the average church member is so vague as to be nearly nonexistent. When he thinks of the matter at all he is likely to try to imagine a nebulous substance like a wisp of invisible smoke which is said to be present in churches and to hover over good people when they are dying. Frankly he does not believe in any such thing, but he wants to believe something, and not feeling up to the task of examining the whole truth in the light of Scripture he compromises by holding belief in the Spirit as far out from the center of his life as possible, letting it make no difference in anything that touches him practically. This describes a surprisingly large number of earnest persons who are sincerely trying to be Christians.

Now, how should we think of the Spirit? A full answer might well run to a dozen volumes. We can at best only point to the "gracious Unction from above" and hope that the reader's own desire may provide the necessary stimulus to urge him on to know the blessed Third Person for himself.

. If I read aright the record of Christian experience through the years, those who most enjoyed the power of the Spirit have had the least to say about Him by way of attempted definition. The Bible saints who walked in the Spirit never tried to explain Him. In post-Biblical times many who were filled and possessed by the Spirit were by the limitations of their literary gifts prevented from telling us much about Him. They had no gift for self-analysis, but lived from within in uncritical simplicity. To them the Spirit was One to be loved and fellowshipped the same as the Lord Jesus Himself. They would have been lost completely in any metaphysical discussion of the nature of the Spirit, but they had no trouble in claiming the power of the Spirit for holy living and fruitful service.

This is as it should be. Personal experience must always be first in real life. The most important thing is that we experience reality by the shortest and most direct method. A child may eat nutritious food without knowing anything about chemistry or diatetics. A country boy may know the delights of pure love while never having heard of Sigmund Freud or Havelock Ellis. Knowledge by acquaintance is always better than mere knowledge by description, and the first does not presuppose the second nor require it.

In religion more than in any other field of human experience a sharp distinction must always be made between *knowing about* and *knowing*. The distinction is the same as between knowing about food and actually eating it. A man can die of starvation knowing all about bread, and a man can remain spiritually dead while knowing all the historic facts of Christianity. "This is life eternal, that they might know thee the only true God, and Jesus Christ, whom thou hast sent." We have but to introduce one extra word into this verse to see how vast is the difference between knowing about and knowing. "This is life eternal, that they might know *about* thee the only true God, and Jesus Christ, whom thou hast sent." That one word makes all the difference between life and death, for it goes to the very root of the verse and changes its theology radically and vitally.

For all this we would not underestimate the importance of mere knowing about. Its value lies in its ability to rouse us to desire to know in actual experience. Thus knowledge by description may lead on to knowledge by acquaintance. *May* lead on, I say, but does not necessarily do so. Thus we dare not conclude that because we learn about the Spirit we for that reason actually know Him. Knowing Him comes only by a personal encounter with the Holy Spirit himself.

How shall we think of the Spirit? A great deal can be learned about the Holy Spirit from the word *spirit* itself. Spirit means existence on a level above and beyond matter; it means life subsisting in another mode. Spirit is substance that has no weight, no dimension, no size nor extension in space. These qualities belong to matter and can have no application to spirit. Yet spirit has true being and is objectively real. If this is hard to visualize, just pass it up, for it is at best but a clumsy attempt of the mind to grasp that which is above the mind's powers. And no harm is done if in our thinking about the Spirit we are forced by the limitations of our intellects to clothe Him in the familiar habiliments of material form.

How shall we think of the Spirit? The Bible and Christian theology agree to teach that He is a Person, endowed with every quality of personality, such as emotion, intellect and will. He knows, He wills, He loves; He feels affection, antipathy and compassion. He thinks, sees, hears and speaks and performs any act of which personality is capable.

One quality belonging to the Holy Spirit, of great interest and importance to every seeking heart, is penetrability. He can penetrate matter, such as the human body; He can penetrate mind; He can penetrate another spirit, such as the human spirit. He can achieve complete penetration of and actual intermingling with the human spirit. He can invade the human heart and make room for Himself without expelling anything essentially human. The integrity of the human personality remains unimpaired. Only moral evil is forced to withdraw.

The metaphysical problem involved here can no more be avoided than it can be solved. How can one personality enter another? The candid reply would be simply that we do not know, but a near approach to an understanding may be made by a simple analogy borrowed from the old devotional writers of several hundred years ago. We place a piece of iron in a fire and blow up the coals. At first we have two distinct substances, iron and fire. When we insert the iron in the fire we achieve the penetration of the fire by the iron. Soon the fire begins to penetrate the iron and we have not only the iron in the fire but the fire in the iron as well. They are two distinct substances, but they have co-mingled and interpenetrated to a point where the two have become one.

In some such manner does the Holy Spirit penetrate our spirits. In the whole experience we remain our very selves. There is no destruction of substance. Each remains a separate being as before; the difference is that now the Spirit penetrates and fills our personalities and we are *experientially one with God.*

How shall we think of the Holy Spirit? The Bible declares that He is God. Every quality belonging to Almighty God is freely attributed to Him. All that God is, the Spirit is declared to be. The Spirit of God is one with and equal to God just as the spirit of a man is equal to and one with the man. This is so fully taught in the Scriptures that we may without loss to the argument omit the formality of proof texts. The most casual reader will have discovered it for himself.

The historic Church when she formulated her "rule of faith" boldly wrote into her confession her belief in the Godhood of the Holy Ghost. The Apostles' Creed witnesses to faith in the Father and in the Son and in the Holy Ghost, and makes no difference between the Three. The Fathers who com-

posed the Nicene Creed testified in a passage of great
beauty to their faith in the deity of the Spirit:

And I believe in the Holy Ghost,
The Lord and Giver of Life,
Who proceedeth from the Father and the Son;
Who with the Father and Son together
Is worshipped and glorified.

The Arian controversy of the Fourth Century
compelled the Fathers to state their beliefs with
greater clarity than before. Among the important
writings which appeared at that time is the Athanasian Creed. Who composed it matters little to us
now. It was written as an attempt to state in as few
words as possible what the Bible teaches about the
nature of God; and this it has done with a compre-
hensiveness and precision hardly matched anywhere
in the literature of the world. Here are a few quota-
tions bearing on the deity of the Holy Ghost:

"There is one Person of the Father, another of
the Son: and another of the Holy Ghost.

But the Godhead of the Father, of the Son, and
of the Holy Ghost, is all one: the Glory equal, the
Majesty co-eternal.

And in this Trinity none is afore, or after other:
none is greater, or less than another;

But the whole three Persons are co-eternal together: and co-equal.

So that in all things, as is aforesaid: the Unity in
Trinity, and Trinity in Unity is to be worshipped."

In her sacred hymnody the Church has freely
acknowledged the Godhead of the Spirit and in her

inspired song she has worshipped Him with joyous abandon. Some of our hymns to the Spirit have become so familiar that we tend to miss their true meaning by the very circumstance of their familiarity. Such a hymn is the wondrous "Holy Ghost, With Light Divine"; another is the more recent "Breathe on Me, Breath of God"; and there are many others. They have been sung so often by persons who have had no experiential knowledge of their content, that for the most of us they have become almost meaningless.

In the poetical works of Frederick Faber I have found a hymn to the Holy Spirit which I would rank among the finest ever written, but so far as I know it has not been set to music, or if it has, it is not sung today in any church with which I am acquainted. Could the reason be that it embodies personal experience of the Holy Spirit so deep, so intimate, so fiery hot that it corresponds to nothing in the hearts of the worshippers in present-day evangelicalism? I quote three stanzas:

> *Fountain of Love! Thyself true God!*
> *Who through eternal days*
> *From Father and from Son hast flowed*
> *In uncreated ways!*
>
> *I dread Thee, Unbegotten Love!*
> *True God! sole Fount of Grace!*
> *And now before Thy blessed throne*
> *My sinful self abase.*
>
> *O Light! O Love! O very God*
> *I dare no longer gaze*

Upon Thy wondrous attributes
And their mysterious ways.

These lines have everything to make a great hymn, sound theology, smooth structure, lyric beauty, high compression of profound ideas and a full charge of lofty religious feeling. Yet they are in complete neglect. I believe that a mighty resurgence of the Spirit's power among us will open again wells of hymnody long forgotten. For song can never bring the Holy Spirit, but the Holy Spirit does invariably bring song. ✓

What we have in the Christian doctrine of the Holy Spirit is Deity present among us. He is not God's messenger only, *He is God.* He is God in contact with His creatures, doing in them and among them a saving and renewing work.

The Persons of the Godhead never work separately. We dare not think of them in such a way as to "divide the substance." Every act of God is done by all three Persons. God is never anywhere present in one Person without the other two. He cannot divide Himself. Where the Spirit is, there also is the Father and the Son. "We will come unto him and make our abode with him." For the accomplishment of some specific work one Person may for the time be more prominent than the others are, but never is He alone. God is altogether present wherever He is present at all.

To the reverent question, "What is God like?" a proper answer will always be, "He is like Christ." For Christ is God, and the Man who walked among men in Palestine was God acting like Himself in the familiar situation where His incarnation placed Him. To the question, "What is the Spirit like?" the answer must always be, "He is like Christ." For the Spirit is the essence of the Father and the Son. As they are, so is He. As we feel toward Christ and toward our Father who art in heaven, so should we feel toward the Spirit of the Father and the Son.

The Holy Spirit is the Spirit of life and light and love. In His uncreated nature He is a boundless sea of fire, flowing, moving ever, performing as He moves the eternal purposes of God. Toward nature He performs one sort of work, toward the world another and toward the Church still another. And every act of His accords with the will of the Triune God. Never does He act on impulse nor move after a quick or arbitrary decision. Since He is the Spirit of the Father He feels toward His people exactly as the Father feels, so there need be on our part no sense of strangeness in His presence. He will always act like Jesus, toward sinners in compassion, toward saints in warm affection, toward human suffering in tenderest pity and love.

It is time for us to repent, for our transgressions against the blessed Third Person have been many and much aggravated. We have bitterly mistreated Him in the house of His friends. We have crucified Him in His own temple as they crucified the Eternal Son on the hill above Jerusalem. And the nails we used were not of iron, but of the finer and more precious stuff of which human life is made. Out of our hearts we took the refined metals of will and feeling and thought, and from them we fashioned the nails of suspicion and rebellion and neglect. By unworthy thoughts about Him and unfriendly attitudes toward Him we grieved and quenched Him days without end.

The truest and most acceptable repentance is to reverse the acts and attitudes of which we repent. A thousand years of remorse over a wrong act would not please God as much as a change of conduct and a reformed life. "Let the wicked forsake his way, and the unrighteous man his thoughts: and let him return unto the Lord, and he will have mercy upon him; and to our God, for he will abundantly pardon."

We can best repent our neglect by neglecting Him no more. Let us begin to think of Him as One to be worshipped and obeyed. Let us throw open every door and invite Him in. Let us surrender to Him every room in the temple of our hearts and insist that He enter and occupy as Lord and Master within His own dwelling. And let us remember that He is drawn to the sweet Name of Jesus as bees are drawn to the fragrance of clover. Where Christ is honored the Spirit is sure to feel welcome; where Christ is glorified He will move about freely, pleased and at home.

VI

The Illumination of the Spirit

JOHN ANSWERED AND SAID, A MAN CAN RECEIVE
NOTHING EXCEPT IT BE GIVEN HIM FROM HEAVEN.

John 3:27

HERE IN A BRIEF sentence is the hope and despair
of mankind. "A man can receive nothing." From
the context we know that John is speaking of spiritual truth. He is telling us that there is a kind of
truth which can never be grasped by the intellect,
for the intellect exists for the apprehension of ideas,
and this truth consists not in ideas but in life. Divine
truth is of the nature of spirit and for that reason
can be received only by spiritual revelation. "Except
it be given him from heaven."

This was no new doctrine which John here set
forth, but an advance rather upon truth already
taught in the Old Testament. The prophet Isaiah,
for instance, has this passage, "My thoughts are not
your thoughts, neither are my ways your ways, saith
the Lord. For as the heavens are higher than the
earth, so are my ways higher than your ways, and my
thoughts than your thoughts." Perhaps this had meant
to its readers no more than that God's thoughts,
while similar to ours, were loftier, and His ways as

high above ours as would befit the ways of One whose
wisdom is infinite and whose power is without
bounds. Now John says plainly enough that God's
thoughts are not only greater than ours quantita-
tively but qualitatively wholly different from ours.
God's thoughts belong to the world of spirit, man's
to the world of intellect, and while spirit can embrace
intellect, the human intellect can never comprehend
spirit. Man's thoughts cannot cross over into God's.
"How unsearchable are his judgments, and his ways
past finding out!"

God made man in His own image and placed
within him an organ by means of which he could
know spiritual things. When man sinned that organ
died. "Dead in sin" is a description not of the body
nor yet of the intellect, but of the organ of God-
knowledge within the human soul. Now men are
forced to depend upon another and inferior organ
and one furthermore which is wholly inadequate to
the purpose. I mean, of course, the mind as the seat
of his powers of reason and understanding.

Man by reason cannot know God; he can only
know about God. Through the light of reason certain important facts about God may be discovered.
"Because that which may be known of God is manifest in them; for God hath showed it unto them. For
the invisible things of him from the creation of the
world are clearly seen, being understood by the
things which are made, even his eternal power and
Godhead; so that they are without excuse." Through
the light of nature man's moral reason may be en-
lightened, but the deeper mysteries of God remain

hidden to him until he has received illumination
from above. "But the natural man receiveth not the
things of the Spirit of God: for they are foolishness
unto him: neither can he know them, because they
are spiritually discerned." When the Spirit illuminates the heart, then a part of the man sees which
never saw before; a part of him knows which never
knew before, and that with a kind of knowing which
the most acute thinker cannot imitate. He knows
now in a deep and authoritative way, and what he
knows needs no reasoned proof. His experience of
knowing is above reason, immediate, perfectly con-
vincing and inwardly satisfying. √

"A man can receive nothing." That is the burden of the Bible. Whatever men may think of human
reason God takes a low view of it. "Where is the
wise? where is the scribe? where is the disputer of
this world? hath not God made foolish the wisdom
of this world?" Man's reason is a fine instrument and
useful within its field. It is a gift of God and God
does not hesitate to appeal to it, as when He cries
to Israel, "Come now, and let us reason together."
The inability of human reason as an organ of divine
knowledge arises not from its own weakness but from
its unfittedness for the task by its own nature. It was
not given as an organ by which to know God.

The doctrine of the inability of the human
mind and the need for divine illumination is so
fully developed in the New Testament that it is nothing short of astonishing that we should have gone
so far astray about the whole thing. Fundamentalism
has stood aloof from the Liberal in self-conscious

superiority and has on its own part fallen into error, the error of textualism, which is simply orthodoxy without the Holy Ghost. Everywhere among Conservatives we find persons who are Bible-taught but not Spirit-taught. They conceive truth to be something which they can grasp with the mind. If a man hold to the fundamentals of the Christian faith he is thought to possess divine truth. But it does not follow. There is no truth apart from the Spirit. The most brilliant intellect may be imbecilic when confronted with the mysteries of God. For a man to understand revealed truth requires an act of God equal to the original act which inspired the text.

"Except it be given him from heaven." Here is the other side of the truth; here is hope for all, for these words do certainly mean that there is such a thing as a gift of knowing, a gift that comes from heaven. Christ taught His disciples to expect the coming of the Spirit of Truth who would teach them all things. He explained Peter's knowledge of His Saviourhood as being a direct revelation from the Father in heaven. And in one of His prayers He said, "I thank thee, O Father, Lord of heaven and earth, because thou hast hidden these things from the wise and prudent, and hast revealed them unto babes." By "the wise and prudent" our Lord meant not Greek philosophers but Jewish Bible students and teachers of the Law.

This basic idea, the inability of human reason as an instrument of God-knowledge, was fully developed in the epistles of Paul. The Apostle frankly rules out every natural faculty as instruments for discovering divine truth and throws us back helpless upon the inworking Spirit. "Eye hath not seen, nor ear heard, neither hath entered into the heart of man, the things which God hath prepared for them that love him. For God hath revealed them unto us by his Spirit: for the Spirit searcheth all things, yea, the deep things of God. For what man knoweth the things of a man, save the spirit of man which is in him? even so the things of God knoweth no man, but the Spirit of God. Now we have received, not the Spirit of the world, but the Spirit which is of God; that we might know the things which are freely given to us of God."

The passage just quoted is taken from Paul's First Epistle to the Corinthians and is not lifted out of context nor placed in a setting which would tend to distort its meaning. Indeed it expresses the very essence of Paul's spiritual philosophy and fully accords with the rest of the Epistle, and I might add, with the rest of Paul's writings as we have them preserved in the New Testament. That type of theological rationalism which is so popular today would have been wholly foreign to the mind of the great Apostle. He had not faith in man's ability to comprehend truth apart from the direct illumination of the Holy Ghost.

I have just now used the word *rationalism* and I must either retract it or justify its use in association with orthodoxy. The latter I think I shall have no trouble doing. For the textualism of our times is based upon the same premise as the old-line rationalism, that is, the belief that the human mind is the supreme authority in the judgment of truth. Or otherwise stated, it is *confidence in the ability of the human mind to do that which the Bible declares it was never created to do and consequently is wholly incapable of doing.* Philosophical rationalism is honest enough to reject the Bible flatly. Theological rationalism rejects it while pretending to accept it and in so doing puts out its own eyes.

The inward kernel of truth has the same configuration as the outward shell. The mind can grasp the shell but only the Spirit of God can lay hold of the internal essence. Our great error has been that we have trusted to the shell and have believed we were sound in the faith because we were able to explain the external shape of truth as found in the letter of the Word. From this mortal error Fundamentalism is slowly dying. We have forgotten that the essence of spiritual truth cannot come to the one who knows the external shell of truth unless there is first a miraculous operation of the Spirit within the heart. Those overtones of religious delight which accompany truth when the Spirit illuminates it are all but missing from the Church today. Those transporting glimpses of the Celestial Country are few and dim; the fragrance of "Sharon's dewy Rose" is hardly discernible. Consequently we have been forced to look elsewhere for our delights and we have found them in the dubious artistry of converted opera singers or the tinkling melodies of odd and curious musical arrangements. We have tried to secure spiritual pleasures by working upon fleshly emotions and whipping up synthetic feeling by means wholly carnal. And the total effect has been evil.

In a remarkable sermon on "The True Way of Attaining Divine Knowledge," John Smith states the truth I am attempting to set forth here. "Were I indeed to define divinity I should rather call it a divine *life* than a divine *science;* it is something rather to be understood by a *spiritual sensation,* than by any *verbal description.* . . . Divinity is indeed a true *efflux* from the eternal Light, which like the sunbeams, does not only enlighten, but *heat* and *enliven.* . . . We must not think that we have attained to the right knowledge of truth, when we have broken through the outward shell of words and phrases that house it up; . . . There is a knowing of Truth as it is in Jesus, as it is in a Christ-like nature, as it is in that sweet, mild, humble, and loving Spirit of Jesus, which spreads itself like a morning sun upon the souls of good men, full of life and light. It profits little to know Christ Himself after the flesh; but he gives his Spirit to good men that search the deep things of God. There is an inward beauty, life and loveliness in divine Truth, which can be known only when it is digested into life and practice."

This old Divine held that a pure life was absolutely necessary to any real understanding of spiritual truth. "There is," he says, "an inward sweetness and deliciousness in divine truth, which no sensual mind can taste or relish: this is that 'natural' man that savors not the things of God . . . Divinity is not so much perceived by a subtle wit as by a purified sense."

Twelve hundred years before these words were uttered Athanasius had written a profound treatise called, "The Incarnation of the Word of God." In this treatise he boldly attacked the difficult problems inherent in the doctrine of the Incarnation. The whole thing is a remarkable demonstration of pure reason engaged with divine revelation. He makes a great case for the deity of Christ, and for all who believe the Bible, settles the matter for all time. Yet so little does he trust the human mind to comprehend divine mysteries that he closes his great work with a strong warning against a mere intellectual understanding of spiritual truth. His words should be printed in large type and tacked on the desk of every pastor and theological student in the world:

"But for the searching of the Scriptures and true knowledge of them, an honorable life is needed, and a pure soul, and that virtue which is according to Christ; so that the intellect guiding its path by it, may be able to attain what it desires, and to comprehend it, in so far as it is accessible to human nature to learn concerning the word of God. For without a pure mind and a modeling of the life after the saints, a man could not possibly comprehend the words of the saints. . . . He that would comprehend the mind of those who speak of God needs begin by washing and cleansing his soul."

The old Jewish believers of pre-Christian times who gave us the (to modern Protestants little-known) books, the Wisdom of Solomon and Ecclesiasticus, believed that it is impossible for an impure heart to know divine truth. "For into a malicious soul wisdom will not enter; nor dwell in the body that is subject unto sin. For the holy spirit of discipline will flee deceit, and remove from thoughts that are without understanding, and will not abide when unrighteousness cometh in."

These books, along with our familiar Book of Proverbs, teach that true spiritual knowledge is the result of a visitation of heavenly wisdom, a kind of baptism of the Spirit of Truth which comes to God-fearing men. This wisdom is always associated with righteousness and humility and is never found apart from godliness and true holiness of life.

Conservative Christians in this day are stumbling over this truth. We need to re-examine the whole thing. We need to learn that truth consists not in correct doctrine, but in correct doctrine *plus the inward enlightenment of the Holy Spirit*. We must declare again the mystery of wisdom from above. A re-preachment of this vital truth could result in a fresh breath from God upon a stale and suffocating orthodoxy.

VII

The Spirit as Power

BUT YE SHALL RECEIVE POWER, AFTER THAT
THE HOLY GHOST IS COME UPON YOU.

Acts 1:8

SOME GOOD CHRISTIANS have misread this text and
have assumed that Christ told his disciples that they
were to receive the Holy Spirit *and* power, the power
to come after the coming of the Spirit. A superficial
reading of the King James text might conceivably
lead to that conclusion, but the truth is that Christ
taught not the coming of the Holy Spirit *and* power,
but the coming of the Holy Spirit *as* power; the
power and the Spirit are the same.

Our mother tongue is a beautiful and facile instrument, but it can also be a tricky and misleading
one, and for this reason it must be used with care
if we would avoid giving and receiving wrong im-
pressions by its means. Especially is this true when
we are speaking of God, for God being wholly unlike
anything or anybody in His universe our very
thoughts of Him as well as our words are in constant
danger of going astray. One example is found in the
words, "The power of God." The danger is that we
think of "power" as something belonging to God as

muscular energy belongs to a man, as something which He *has* and which might be separated from Him and still have existence in itself. We must remember that the "attributes" of God are not component parts of the blessed Godhead nor elements out of which He is composed. A god who could be *composed* would not be God at all but the work of something or someone greater than he, great enough to compose him. We would then have a synthetic God made out of the pieces we call attributes, and the true God would be another Being altogether, One indeed who is above all thought and all conceiving.

The Bible and Christian theology teach that God is an indivisible Unity, being what He is in undivided oneness, from Whom nothing can be taken and to Whom nothing can be added. Mercy, for instance, immutability, eternity, these are but names which we have given to something which God has declared to be true of Himself. All the "of God" expressions in the Bible must be understood to mean not what God has but *what God is* in His undivided and indivisible Unity. Even the word "nature" when applied to God should be understood as an accommodation to our human way of looking at things and not as an accurate description of anything true of the mysterious Godhead. God has said, "I am that I am," and we can only repeat in reverence, "O God, Thou art."

Our Lord before His ascension said to His disciples, "Tarry in the city of Jerusalem until ye be endued with power from on high." That word *until* is a time-word; it indicates a point in relation to which everything is either before or after. So the experience of those disciples could be stated like this: Up to that point they *had not* received the power; at that point they *did* receive the power; after that point they *had* received the power. Such is the plain historic fact. Power came upon the Church, such power as had never been released into human nature before (with the lone exception of that mighty anointing which came upon Christ at the waters of Jordan). That power, still active in the Church, has enabled her to exist for nearly twenty centuries, even though for all of that time she has remained a highly unpopular minority group among the nations of mankind and has always been surrounded by enemies who would gladly have ended her existence if they could have done so.

"Ye shall receive power." By those words our Lord raised the expectation of His disciples and taught them to look forward to the coming of a supernatural potency into their natures from a source outside of themselves. It was to be something previously unknown to them, but suddenly to come upon them from another world. It was to be nothing less than God himself entering into them with the purpose of ultimately reproducing His own likeness within them.

Here is the dividing line that separates Christianity from all occultism and from every kind of oriental cult ancient or modern. These all are built around the same ideas, varying only in minor details, each with its own peculiar set of phrases and apparently vying with each other in vagueness and obscurity. They each advise, "Get in tune with the Infinite," or "Wake the giant within you," or "Tune in to your hidden potentialities," or "Learn to think creatively." All this may have some fleeting value as a psychological shot in the arm, but its results are not permanent because at its best it builds its hopes upon the fallen nature of man and knows no invasion from above. And whatever may be said in its favor, *it most certainly is not Christianity*.

Christianity takes for granted the absence of any self-help and offers a power which is nothing less than the power of God. This power is to come upon powerless men as a gentle but resistless invasion from another world bringing a moral potency infinitely beyond anything that might be stirred up from within. This power is sufficient; no additional help is needed, no auxiliary source of spiritual energy, for it is the Holy Spirit of God come where the weakness lay to supply power and grace to meet the moral need.

Set over against such a mighty provision as this ethical Christianity (if I may be allowed the term) is seen to be no Christianity at all. An infantile copying of Christ's "ideals," a pitiable effort to carry out the teachings of the Sermon on the Mount! All this is but religious child's play and is not the faith of Christ and the New Testament.

"Ye shall receive power." This was and is a unique afflatus, an enduement of supernatural energy affecting every department of the believer's life and remaining with him forever. It is not physical power nor even mental power though it may touch everything both mental and physical in its benign out-workings. It is too another kind of power than that seen in nature, in the lunar attraction that creates the tides or the angry flash that splits the great oak during a storm. This power from God operates on another level and affects another department of His wide creation. It is spiritual power. It is the kind of power that God is. It is the ability to achieve spiritual and moral ends. Its long range result is to produce God-like character in men and women who were once wholly evil by nature and by choice.

Now how does this power operate? At its purest it is an unmediated force directly applied by the Spirit of God to the spirit of man. The wrestler achieves his ends by the pressure of his physical body upon the body of his opponent, the teacher by the pressure of ideas upon the mind of the student, the moralist by the pressure of duty upon the conscience of the disciple. So the Holy Spirit performs His blessed work by direct contact with the human spirit.

It would be less than accurate to say that the power of God is always experienced in a direct and unmediated form, for when He so wills the Spirit may use other means as Christ used spittle to heal a blind man. But always the power is above and beyond the means. While the Spirit may use appropriate means to bless a believing man, He never need do so for they are at best but temporary concessions made to our ignorance and unbelief. Where adequate power is present almost any means will suffice, but where the power is absent not all the means in the world can secure the desired end. The Spirit of

God may use a song, a sermon, a good deed, a text or the mystery and majesty of nature, but always the final work will be done by the pressure of the inliving Spirit upon the human heart.

In the light of this it will be seen how empty and meaningless is the average church service today. All the means are in evidence; the one ominous weakness is the absence of the Spirit's power. The form of godliness is there, and often the form is perfected till it is an aesthetic triumph. Music and poetry, art and oratory, symbolic vesture and solemn tones combine to charm the mind of the worshipper, but too often the supernatural afflatus is not there. The power from on high is neither known nor desired by pastor or people. This is nothing less than tragic, and all the more so because it falls within the field of religion where the eternal destinies of men are involved.

To the absence of the Spirit may be traced that vague sense of unreality which almost everywhere invests religion in our times. In the average church service the most real thing is the shadowy unreality of everything. The worshipper sits in a state of suspended mentation; a kind of dreamy numbness creeps upon him; he hears words but they do not register, he cannot relate them to anything on his own life-level. He is conscious of having entered a kind of half-world; his mind surrenders itself to a more or less pleasant mood which passes with the benediction leaving no trace behind. It does not affect anything in his everyday life. He is aware of no power, no Presence, no spiritual reality. There is simply nothing in his experience corresponding to the things which he heard from the pulpit or sang in the hymns.

One meaning of the word "power" is "ability to do." There precisely is the wonder of the Spirit's work in the Church and in the hearts of Christians, His sure ability to make spiritual things real to the soul. This power can go straight to its object with piercing directness; it can diffuse itself through the mind like an infinitely fine volatile essence securing ends above and beyond the limits of the intellect. Reality is its subject matter, reality in heaven and upon earth. It does not create objects which are not there but reveals objects already present and hidden from the soul. In actual human experience this is likely to be the first felt in a heightened sense of the Presence of Christ. He is felt to be a real Person and to be intimately, ravishingly near. Then all other spiritual objects begin to stand out clearly before the mind. Grace, forgiveness, cleansing take on a form of almost bodily clearness. Prayer loses its unmeaning quality and becomes a sweet conversation with Someone actually there. Love for God and for the children of God takes possession of the soul. We feel ourselves near to heaven and it is now the earth and the world that begin to seem unreal. We know them now for what they are, realities indeed, but like stage scenery here for one brief hour and soon to pass away. The world to come takes on a hard outline before our minds and begins to invite our interest and our devotion. Then the whole life changes to suit the new reality and the change is permanent. Slight fluctuations there may be like the rise and dip of the line on a graph, but the established direction is upward and the ground taken is held.

This is not all, but it will give a fair idea of what is meant when the New Testament speaks of *power,* and perhaps by contrast we may learn how little of the power we enjoy.

I think there can be no doubt that the need above all other needs in the Church of God at this moment is the power of the Holy Spirit. More education, better organization, finer equipment, more advanced methods—all are unavailing. It is like bringing a better Pulmotor after the patient is dead. Good as these things are they can never give life. "It is the Spirit that quickeneth." Good as they are they can never bring power. "Power belongeth unto God." Protestantism is on the wrong road when it tries to win merely by means of a "united front." It is not organizational unity we need most; the great need is power. The headstones in the cemetery present a united front, but they stand mute and helpless while the world passes by.

I suppose my suggestion will not receive much serious attention, but I should like to suggest that we Bible-believing Christians announce a moratorium on religious activity and set our house in order preparatory to the coming of an afflatus from above. So carnal is the body of Christians which composes the conservative wing of the Church, so shockingly irreverent are our public services in some quarters, so degraded are our religious tastes in still others, that the need for power could scarcely have been greater at any time in history. I believe we should profit immensely were we to declare a period of silence and self-examination during which each one of us searched his own heart and sought to meet every condition for a real baptism of power from on high.

We may be sure of one thing, that for our deep trouble there is no cure apart from a visitation, yes, an *invasion* of power from above. Only the Spirit Himself can show us what is wrong with us and only the Spirit can prescribe the cure. Only the Spirit can save us from the numbing unreality of Spiritless Christianity. Only the Spirit can show us the Father and the Son. Only the inworking of the Spirit's power can discover to us the solemn majesty and the heart ravishing mystery of the Triune God.

VIII

The Holy Spirit as Fire

AND THERE APPEARED UNTO THEM
CLOVEN TONGUES LIKE AS OF FIRE,
AND IT SAT UPON EACH OF THEM.
Acts 2:3

CHRISTIAN THEOLOGY TEACHES that God in His essential nature is both inscrutable and ineffable. This by simple definition means that He is incapable of being searched into or understood, and that He cannot tell forth or utter what He is. This inability lies not in God but in the limitations of our creaturehood. "Why inquirest thou after my name, for it is secret?" Only God knows God in any final meaning of the word *know*. "Even so the things of God knoweth no man, but the Spirit of God."

To the average Christian today this may sound strange, if not downright confusing, for the temper of religious thinking in our times is definitely not theological. We may live out a full lifetime and die without once having our minds challenged by the sweet mystery of the Godhead if we depend upon the churches to do the challenging. They are altogether too busy playing with shadows and getting "adjusted" to one thing and another to spend much time think-

94

ing about God. It might be well, therefore, to consider for a moment longer the divine inscrutability.

God in His essential Being is unique in the only sense that word will bear. That is, there is nothing like Him in the universe. What He is cannot be conceived by the mind because He is "altogether other" than anything with which we have had experience before. The mind has no material with which to start. No man has ever entertained a thought which can be said to describe God in any but the vaguest and most imperfect sense. Where God is known at all it must be otherwise than by our creature-reason.

Novatian, in a famous treatise on the Trinity written sometime about the middle of the third century, says, "In all our meditations upon the qualities of the attributes and content of God, we pass beyond our powers of fit conception, nor can human eloquence put forth a power commensurate with His greatness. At the contemplation and utterance of His majesty, all eloquence is rightly dumb, all mental effort is feeble. For God is greater than mind itself. His greatness cannot be conceived. Nay, if we could conceive of His greatness, He would be less than the human mind which could form the conception. He is greater than all language, and no statement can express Him. Indeed, if any statement could express Him, He would be less than human speech, which could by such statement comprehend and gather up all that He is. Up to a certain point, of course, we can have experience of Him, without language, but no man can express in words all that He is in Himself. Suppose, for instance, one speaks of Him as light; this is an account of part of His creation, not of Himself. It does not express what He is. Or suppose one speaks of Him as power. This too sets forth in words His attribute of might, rather than His being. Or suppose one speaks of Him as majesty. Once again, we have a declaration of the honor which is His Own, rather than of Him in Himself. . . . To sum up the matter in a single sentence, every possible statement that can be made about God expresses some possession or virtue of God, rather than God Himself. What words or thoughts are worthy of Him, Who is above all language and all thought? The conception of God as He is can only be grasped in one way, and even that is impossible for us, beyond our grasp and understanding; by thinking of Him as a Being Whose attributes and greatness are beyond our powers of understanding, or even of thought."

Just because God cannot tell us *what He is* He very often tells us *what He is like*. By these "like" figures He leads our faltering minds as close as they can come to that "Light which no man can approach unto." Through the more cumbersome medium of the intellect the soul is prepared for the moment when it can, through the operation of the Holy Spirit, know God as He is in Himself. God has used a number of these similitudes to hint at His incomprehensible being, and judging from the Scriptures one would gather that *His favorite similitude is fire*. In one place the Spirit speaks expressly, "For our God is a consuming fire." This accords with His revelation of Himself as recorded throughout the

Bible. As a fire He spoke to Moses from the burning bush; in the fire He dwelt above the camp of Israel through all the wilderness journey; as fire He dwelt between the wings of the cherubim in the Holy of Holies; to Ezekiel He revealed Himself as a strange brightness of "a fire infolding itself." "I saw as it were the appearance of a fire and it had a brightness round about. As the appearance of the bow that is in the cloud in the day of rain, so was the appearance of the brightness round about. This was the appearance of the likeness of the glory of the Lord. And when I saw it, I fell on my face, and I heard a voice of one that spake" (Ezekiel 1:27-28).

With the coming of the Holy Spirit at Pentecost the same imagery was continued. "And there appeared unto them cloven tongues like as of fire, and it sat upon each of them." That which came upon the disciples in that upper room was nothing less than God Himself. To their mortal eyes He appeared as fire, and may we not safely conclude that those Scripture-taught believers knew at once what it meant? The God who had appeared to them as fire throughout all their long history was now dwelling in them as fire. He had moved from without to the interior of their lives. The Shekinah that had once blazed over the mercy seat now blazed on their foreheads as an external emblem of the fire that had invaded their natures. This was Deity giving Himself to ransomed men. The flame was the seal of a new union. They were now men and women of the Fire.

Here is the whole final message of the New Testament: Through the atonement in Jesus' blood

sinful men may now become one with God. Deity
indwelling men! That is Christianity in its fullest
effectuation, and even those greater glories of the
world to come will be in essence but a greater and
more perfect experience of the soul's union with God.

Deity indwelling men! That, I say, is Christianity, and no man has experienced rightly the power
of Christian belief until he has known this for himself as a living reality. Everything else is preliminary
to this. Incarnation, atonement, justification, regeneration; what are these but acts of God preparatory
to the work of invading and the act of indwelling
the redeemed human soul? Man who moved out of
the heart of God by sin now moves back into the
heart of God by redemption. God who moved out
of the heart of man because of sin now enters again
His ancient dwelling to drive out His enemies and
once more make the place of His feet glorious.

That visible fire on the day of Pentecost had for
the Church a deep and tender significance, for it told
to all ages that they upon whose heads it sat were men
and women apart; they were "creatures out of the
fire" as surely as were they whom Ezekiel in his vision
saw by the river Chebar. The mark of the fire was
the sign of divinity; they who received it were forever a peculiar people, sons and daughters of the
Flame.

One of the most telling blows which the enemy
ever struck at the life of the Church was to create in
her a fear of the Holy Spirit. No one who mingles
with Christians in these times will deny that such
a fear exists. Few there are who without restraint

will open their whole heart to the blessed Comforter. He has been and is so widely misunderstood that the very mention of His Name in some circles is enough to frighten many people into resistance. The source of this unreasoning fear may easily be traced, but it would be a fruitless labor to do it here. Sufficient to say that the fear is groundless. Perhaps we may help to destroy its power over us if we examine that fire which is the symbol of the Spirit's Person and Presence.

The Holy Spirit is first of all *a moral flame*. It is not an accident of language that He is called the *Holy* Spirit, for whatever else the word *holy* may mean it does undoubtedly carry with it the idea of moral purity. And the Spirit, being God, must be absolutely and infinitely pure. With Him there are not (as with men) grades and degrees of holiness. He is holiness itself, the sum and essence of all that is unspeakably pure.

No one whose senses have been exercised to know good and evil but must grieve over the sight of zealous souls seeking to be filled with the Holy Spirit while they are yet living in a state of moral carelessness or borderline sin. Such a thing is a moral contradiction. Whoever would be filled and indwelt by the Spirit should first judge his life for any hidden iniquities; he should courageously expel from his heart everything which is out of accord with the character of God as revealed by the Holy Scriptures.

At the base of all true Christian experience must lie a sound and sane morality. No joys are valid, no delights legitimate where sin is allowed to live in

life or conduct. No transgression of pure righteousness dare excuse itself on the ground of superior
religious experience. To seek high emotional states
while living in sin is to throw our whole life open to
self deception and the judgment of God. "Be ye
holy" is not a mere motto to be framed and hung on
the wall. It is a serious commandment from the Lord
of the whole earth. "Cleanse your hands, ye sinners;
and purify your hearts, ye double minded. Be afflicted, and mourn, and weep: let your laughter be
turned into mourning, and your joy into heaviness"
(James 4:8-9). The true Christian ideal is not to be
happy but to be holy. The holy heart alone can be
the habitation of the Holy Ghost.

The Holy Spirit is also a *spiritual flame*. He
alone can raise our worship to true spiritual levels.
For we might as well know once for all that morality
and ethics, however lofty, are still not Christianity.
The faith of Christ undertakes to raise the soul to
actual communion with God, to introduce into our
religious experiences a supra-rational element as far
above mere goodness as the heavens are above the
earth. The coming of the Spirit brought to the Book
of Acts this very quality of supramundaneness, this
mysterious elevation of tone not found in as high
intensity even in the Gospels. The key of the Book
of Acts is definitely the major. There is in it no
trace of creature-sadness, no lingering disappointment, no quaver of uncertainty. The mood is heavenly. A victorious spirit is found there, a spirit
which could never be the result of mere religious
belief. The joy of the first Christians was not the joy

of logic working on facts. They did not reason, "Christ is risen from the dead; therefore we ought to be glad." Their gladness was as great a miracle as the resurrection itself; indeed these were and are organically related. The moral happiness of the Creator had taken residence in the breasts of redeemed creatures and they could not but be glad.

The flame of the Spirit is also *intellectual*. Reason, say the theologians, is one of the divine attributes. There need be no incompatibilty between the deepest experiences of the Spirit and the highest attainments of the human intellect. *It is only required that the Christian intellect be fully surrendered to God and there need be no limit to its activities* beyond those imposed upon it by its own strength and size. How cold and deadly is the unblessed intellect. A superior brain without the saving essence of godliness may turn against the human race and drench the world with blood, or worse, it may loose ideas into the earth which will continue to curse mankind for centuries after it has turned to dust again. But a Spirit-filled mind is a joy to God and a delight to all men of good will. What would the world have missed if it had been deprived of the love-filled mind of a David or a John or an Isaac Watts?

We naturally shy away from superlatives and from comparisons which praise one virtue at the expense of another, yet I wonder whether there is on earth anything as exquisitely lovely as a brilliant mind aglow with the love of God. Such a mind sheds a mild and healing ray which can actually be *felt* by those who come near it. Virtue goes forth from it and blesses those who merely touch the hem of its garment. One has, for instance, but to read *The Celestial Country,* by Bernard of Cluny, to understand what I mean. There a sensitive and shining intellect warm with the fire of the inliving Spirit writes with a vast and tender sympathy of those longings for immortality which have dwelt deep in the human breast since the first man kneeled down upon the earth out of whose bosom he came and into whose bosom he must soon return again. For loftiness of concept, for sheer triumph of the Christian spirit over mortality, for ability to rest the soul and raise the mind to rapturous worship its equal is hardly found anywhere in uninspired literature. I submit it as my respectful opinion that this single hymn may have ministered more healing virtue to distressed spirits than all the writings of secular poets and philosophers since the art of writing was invented. No unblessed intellect, however sure its genius, would be remotely capable of producing such a work. One closes the book after reading it with the feeling, yes the solemn conviction, that he has heard the voice of the cherubim and the sound of harpers strumming beside the sea of God.

This same feeling of near-inspiration is experienced also in the letters of Samuel Rutherford, in the *Te Deum,* in many of the hymns of Watts and Wesley, and occasionally in a work of some lesser known saint whose limited gifts may have been for one joyous moment made incandescent by the fire of the indwelling Spirit.

The blight of the Pharisee's heart in olden times was doctrine without love. With the teachings of the Pharisees Christ had little quarrel, but with the pharisaic spirit He carried on unceasing warfare to the end. It was religion that put Christ on the cross, religion without the indwelling Spirit. It is no use to deny that Christ was crucified by persons who would today be called Fundamentalists. This should prove most disquieting if not downright distressing to us who pride ourselves on our orthodoxy. An unblessed soul filled with the letter of truth may actually be worse off than a pagan kneeling before a fetish. We are safe only when the love of God is shed abroad in our hearts by the Holy Ghost, only when our intellects are indwelt by the loving Fire that came at Pentecost. For the Holy Spirit is not a luxury, not something added now and again to produce a de luxe type of Christian once in a generation. No, He is for every child of God a vital necessity, and that He fill and indwell His people is more than a languid hope. It is rather an inescapable imperative.

The Spirit is also a *volitional flame*. Here as elsewhere the imagery is inadequate to express all the truth, and unless care is taken we may easily gain a wrong impression from its use. For fire as we see and know it every day is a *thing*, not a person, and for that reason it has no will of its own. But the Holy Spirit is a Person, having those attributes of personality of which volition is one. He does not, upon entering the human soul, void any of His attributes, nor does He surrender them in part or in full to the soul into which He enters. Remember, the Holy

Spirit is Lord. "Now the Lord is that Spirit," said Paul to the Corinthians. The Nicene Creed says, "And I believe in the Holy Ghost, the Lord and Giver of Life," and the Athanasian Creed declares, "So likewise the Father is Lord, the Son Lord, and the Holy Ghost Lord. And yet not three Lords: but one Lord." Whatever problems this may pose for the understanding, our faith must accept it and make it a part of our total belief about God and the Spirit. Now it hardly need be said that the Sovereign Lord will never abandon the prerogatives of His Godhood. Wherever He is He must continue to act like Himself. When He enters the human heart He will be there what He has always been, Lord in His own right.

The deep disease of the human heart is a will broken loose from its center, like a planet which has left its central sun and started to revolve around some strange body from outer space which may have moved in close enough to draw it away. When Satan said, "I will," he broke loose from his normal center, and the disease with which he has infected the human race is the disease of disobedience and revolt. Any adequate scheme of redemption must take into account this revolt and must undertake to restore again the human will to its proper place in the will of God. In accord with this underlying need for the healing of the will, the Holy Spirit, when He effects His gracious invasion of the believing heart, must win that heart to glad and voluntary obedience to the whole will of God. The cure must be wrought from within; no outward conformity will do. Until the will is sanctified the man is still a rebel, just as an outlaw is still an outlaw at heart even though he may be yielding grudging obedience to the sheriff who is taking him to prison.

The Holy Spirit achieves this inward cure by merging the will of the redeemed man with His own. This is not accomplished at one stroke. There must be, it is true, some kind of over-all surrender of the will to Christ before any work of grace can be done, but the full mergence of every part of the life with the life of God in the Spirit is likely to be a longer process than we in our creature impatience would wish. The most advanced soul may be shocked and chagrined to discover some private area within his life where he had been, unknown to himself, acting as lord and proprietor of that which he thought he had given to God. It is the work of the in-living Spirit to point out these moral discrepancies and correct them. He does not, as is sometimes said, "break" the human will, but He does invade it and bring it gently to a joyous union with the will of God.

To will the will of God is to do more than give unprotesting consent to it; it is rather to choose God's will with positive determination. As the work of God advances the Christian finds himself free to choose whatever he will, and he gladly chooses the will of God as his highest conceivable good. Such a man has found life's highest goal. He has been placed beyond the little disappointments that plague the rest of men. Whatever happens to him is the will of God for him and that is just what he most ardently desires. But it is only fair to state that this condition is one not reached by many of the busy Christians of our busy times. Until it is reached, however, the Christian's peace cannot be complete. There must be still a certain inward controversy, a sense of spiritual disquiet which poisons our joy and greatly reduces our power.

Another quality of the in-dwelling Fire is *emotion*. This must be understood in the light of what has been said before about the divine inscrutability. What God is in His unique essence cannot be discovered by the mind nor uttered by the lips, but those qualities in God which may be termed rational, and so received by the intellect, have been freely set forth in the sacred Scriptures. They do not tell us what God is, but they do tell us what God is like, and the sum of them constitute a mental picture of the Divine Being seen as it were afar off and through a glass darkly.

Now the Bible teaches that there is something in God which is like emotion. He experiences something which is like our love, something that is like our grief, that is like our joy. And we need not fear to go along with this conception of what God is like. Faith would easily draw the inference that since we were made in His image He would have qualities like our own. But such an inference, while satisfying to the mind, is not the ground of our belief. *God has said certain things about Himself, and these furnish all the grounds we require.* "The Lord thy God in the midst of thee is mighty; he will save, he will rejoice over thee with joy; he will rest in his love, he will joy over thee with singing" (Zephaniah 3:17).

This is but one verse among thousands which serve to form our rational picture of what God is like, and they tell us plainly that God feels something like our love, like our joy, and what He feels makes Him act very much as we would in a similar situation; He rejoices over His loved ones with joy and singing.

Here is emotion on as high a plane as it can ever be seen, emotion flowing out of the heart of God Himself. Feeling, then, is not the degenerate son of unbelief that it is often painted by some of our Bible teachers. Our ability to feel is one of the marks of our divine origin. We need not be ashamed of either tears or laughter. The Christian stoic who has crushed his feelings is only two-thirds of a man; an important third part has been repudiated.

Holy feeling had an important place in the life of our Lord. "For the joy that was set before Him" He endured the cross and despised its shame. He pictured Himself crying, "Rejoice with me, for I have found my sheep which was lost." On the night of His agony He "sang an hymn" before going out to the Mount of Olives. After His resurrection He sang among His brethren in the great congregation (Psalm 22:22). And if the Song of Solomon refers to Christ (as most Christians believe it does) then how are we to miss the sound of His rejoicing as He brings His bride home after the night has ended and the shadows have fled away?

One of the very greatest calamities which sin has brought upon us is the debasement of our normal emotions. We laugh at things which are not funny; we find pleasure in acts which are beneath our human dignity; and we rejoice in objects which should have no place in our affections. The objection to "sinful pleasures" which has always been characteristic of the true saint, is at bottom simply a protest against the degradation of our human emotions. That gambling, for instance, should be allowed to engross the interests of men made in the image of God has seemed like a horrible perversion of noble powers; that alcohol should be necessary to stimulate the feeling of pleasure has seemed like a kind of prostitution; that men should turn to the man-made theatre for enjoyment has seemed an affront to the God who placed us in the midst of a universe charged with high dramatic action. The world's artificial pleasures are all but evidence that the human race has to a large extent lost its power to enjoy the true pleasures of life and is forced to substitute for them false and degrading thrills.

The work of the Holy Spirit is, among other things, to rescue the redeemed man's emotions, to restring his harp and open again the wells of sacred joy which have been stopped up by sin. That He does this is the unanimous testimony of the saints. And it is not inconsistent with the whole way of God in His creation. Pure pleasure is a part of life, such an important part that it is difficult to see how human life could be justified if it were to consist of endless existence devoid of pleasurable feeling.

The Holy Spirit would set an aeolian harp in the window of our souls so that the winds of heaven may play sweet melody for a musical accompaniment to the humblest task we may be called to perform. The spiritual love of Christ will make constant music within our hearts and enable us to rejoice even in our sorrows.

IX

Why the World Cannot Receive

THE SPIRIT OF TRUTH; WHOM
THE WORLD CANNOT RECEIVE.
John 14:17

THE CHRISTIAN FAITH, based upon the New Testament, teaches the complete antithesis between the Church and the world. I have noted this briefly in a previous chapter, but the matter is so important to the seeking soul that I feel that I must here go into the whole thing a little further.

It is no more than a religious platitude to say that the trouble with us today is that we have tried to bridge the gulf between two opposites, the world and the Church, and have performed an illicit marriage for which there is no biblical authority. Actually no real union between the world and the Church is possible. When the Church joins up with the world it is the true Church no longer but only a pitiful hybrid thing, an object of smiling contempt to the world and an abomination to the Lord.

The twilight in which many (or should we say *most?*) believers walk today is not caused by any vagueness on the part of the Bible. Nothing could be clearer than the pronouncements of the Scriptures on the Christian's relation to the world. The confusion which gathers around this matter results from the unwillingness of professing Christians to take the Word of the Lord seriously. Christianity is so entangled with the world that millions never guess how radically they have missed the New Testament pattern. Compromise is everywhere. The world is whitewashed just enough to pass inspection by blind men posing as believers, and those same believers are everlastingly seeking to gain acceptance with the world. By mutual concessions men who call themselves Christians manage to get on with men who have for the things of God nothing but quiet contempt.

This whole thing is spiritual in its essence. A Christian is what he is not by ecclesiastical manipulation but by the new birth. He is a Christian because of a Spirit which dwells in him. Only that which is born of the Spirit is spirit. The flesh can never be converted into spirit, no matter how many church dignitaries work on it. Confirmation, baptism, holy communion, confession of faith: none of these nor all of them together can turn flesh into spirit nor make of a son of Adam a son of God. "Because ye are sons," wrote Paul to the Galatians, "God hath sent forth the Spirit of his Son into your hearts, crying, Abba, Father." And to the Corinthians he wrote, "Examine yourselves, whether ye be in the faith; prove your own selves. Know ye not your own selves, how that Jesus Christ is in you, except ye be reprobates?" And to the Romans, "But ye are not in the flesh, but in the Spirit, if so be that the Spirit of God dwell in you. Now if any man have not the Spirit of Christ he is none of his."

That terrible zone of confusion so evident in the whole life of the Christian community could be cleared up in one day if the followers of Christ would begin to follow Christ instead of each other. For our Lord was very plain in His teaching about the believer and the world.

On one occasion, after receiving unsolicited and carnal advice from sincere but unenlightened brethren, our Lord replied, "My time is not yet come: but your time is always ready. The world cannot hate you, but me it hateth, because I testify of it that the works thereof are evil." He identified His fleshly brethren with the world and said that they and He were of two different spirits. The world hated Him but could not hate them because it could not hate itself. A house divided against itself cannot stand. Adam's house must remain loyal to itself or it will tear itself apart. Though the sons of the flesh may quarrel among themselves they are at bottom one with each other. It is when the Spirit of God comes in that an alien element has entered. "If the world hate you," said the Lord to His disciples, "ye know that it hated me before it hated you. If ye were of the world, the world would love his own: but because ye are not of the world, but I have chosen you out of the world, therefore the world hateth you." Paul explained to the Galatians the difference between the bond child and the free: "But as then he that was born after the flesh persecuted him that was born after the Spirit, even so it is now" (Galatians 4:29).

So throughout the entire New Testament a sharp line is drawn between the Church and the world. There is no middle ground. The Lord recognizes no good natured "agreeing to disagree" so that the followers of the Lamb may adopt the world's ways and travel along the world's path. The gulf between the true Christian and the world is as great as that which separated the rich man and Lazarus. And, furthermore, it is the same gulf, that is, it is the gulf that divides the world of ransomed from the world of fallen men.

I well know, and feel deeply, how offensive such teaching as this must be to that great flock of worldlings which mills around the traditional sheepfold. I cannot hope to escape the charge of bigotry and intolerance which will undoubtedly be brought against me by the confused religionists who seek to make themselves sheep by association. But we may as well face the hard truth that men do not become Christians by associating with church people, nor by religious contact, nor by religious education; they become Christians only by an invasion of their nature by the Spirit of God in the New Birth. And when they do thus become Christians they are immediately members of a new race, "a chosen generation, a royal priesthood, an holy nation, a peculiar people . . . which in times past were not a people, but are now the people of God: which had not obtained mercy, but now have obtained mercy" (1 Peter 2:9-10).

In the verses quoted there has been no wish to quote out of context nor to focus attention upon one side of truth to draw it away from another. The teaching of these passages is altogether one with all New Testament truth. It is as if we dipped a cup of water from the sea. What we took out would not be all the water in the ocean, but it would be a true sample and would perfectly agree with the rest.

The difficulty we modern Christians face is not misunderstanding the Bible, but persuading our untamed hearts to accept its plain instructions. Our problem is to get the consent of our world-loving minds to make Jesus Lord in fact as well as in word. For it is one thing to say, "Lord, Lord," and quite another thing to obey the Lord's commandments. We may sing, "Crown Him Lord of all," and rejoice in the tones of the loud-sounding organ and the deep melody of harmonious voices, but still we have done nothing until we have left the world and set our faces toward the city of God in hard practical reality. When faith becomes obedience then it is true faith indeed.

The world's spirit is strong, and it clings to us as close as the smell of smoke to our garments. It can change its face to suit any circumstance and so deceive many a simple Christian whose senses are not exercised to discern good and evil. It can play at religion with every appearance of sincerity. It can have fits of conscience (particularly during Lent) and even confess its evil ways in the public press. It will praise religion and fawn on the Church for its ends. It will contribute to charitable causes and promote campaigns to furnish clothing for the poor. *Only let Christ keep His distance and never assert His Lord-*

ship over it. This it will positively not endure. And toward the true Spirit of Christ it will show only antagonism. The world's press (which is always its real mouthpiece) will seldom give a child of God a fair deal. If the facts compel a favorable report, the tone is apt to be condescending and ironic. The note of contempt sounds through.

Both the sons of this world and the sons of God have been baptized into a spirit, but the spirit of the world and the Spirit which dwells in the hearts of twice-born men are as far apart as heaven and hell. Not only are they the complete opposite of each other but they are sharply antagonistic to each other as well. To a son of earth the things of the Spirit are either ridiculous, in which case he is amused, or they are meaningless, in which case he is bored. "But the natural man receiveth not the things of the Spirit of God: for they are foolishness unto him: neither can he know them, because they are spiritually discerned."

In the First Epistle of John two words are used over and over, the words *they* and *ye,* and they designate two wholly different worlds. *They* refers to the men and women of Adam's fallen world; *ye* refers to the chosen ones who have left all to follow Christ. The apostle does not genuflect to the little god Tolerance (the worship of which has become in America a kind of secondary surface religion); he is bluntly intolerant. He knows that tolerance may be merely another name for indifference. It takes a vigorous faith to accept the teaching of the man John. It is so much easier to blur the lines of separation and so offend no one. Pious generalities and the use of *we* to mean both Christians and unbelievers is much safer. The fatherhood of God can be stretched to include everyone from Jack the Ripper to Daniel the Prophet. Thus no one is offended and everyone feels quite snug and ready for heaven. But the man who laid his ear on Jesus' breast was not so easily deceived. He drew a line to divide the race of men into two camps, to separate the saved from the lost, those who shall rise to eternal reward from them that shall sink to final despair. On one side are *they* that know not God; on the other *ye* (or with a change of person, *we*), and between the two is a moral gulf too wide for any man to cross.

Here is the way John states it: "Ye are of God, little children, and have overcome them: because greater is he that is in you than he that is in the world. They are of the world: therefore speak they of the world, and the world heareth them. We are of God: he that knoweth God heareth us; he that is not of God heareth not us. Hereby know we the spirit of truth and the spirit of error." Such language as this is too plain to confuse anyone who honestly wants to know the truth. Our problem is not one of understanding, I repeat, but of faith and obedience. The question is not a theological one, What does this teach? It is a moral one, Am I willing to accept this and abide by its consequences? Can I endure the cold stare? Have I the courage to stand up to the slashing attack of the "liberal"? Dare I invite the hate of men who will be affronted by my attitude? Have I independence of mind sufficient to challenge the opinions of popular religion and go along with an apostle? Or briefly, can I bring myself to take up the cross with its blood and is reproach?

The Christian is called to separation from the world, but we must be sure we know what we mean (or more important, what God means) by the *world*. We are likely to make it mean something external only and thus miss its real meaning. The theatre, cards, liquor, gambling: these are not the world; they are merely an external manifestation of the world. Our warfare is not against mere worldly ways, but against the *spirit* of the world. For man, whether he is saved or lost, is essentially spirit. The world, in the New Testament meaning of the word, is simply unregenerate human nature wherever it is found, whether in a tavern or in a church. Whatever springs out of, is built upon or receives support from fallen human nature is the world, whether it is morally base or morally respectable. The ancient Pharisees, in spite of their zealous devotion to religion, were of the very essence of the world. The spiritual principles upon which they built their system were drawn not from above but from below. They employed against Jesus the tactics of men. They bribed men to tell lies in defense of truth. To defend God they acted like devils. To support the Bible they defied the teachings of the Bible. They scuttled religion to save religion. They gave rein to blind hate in the name of the religion of love. There we see the world in all of its grim defiance of God. So fierce was this spirit that it never rested till it had put to death the Son of God Himself. The spirit of the Pharisees was actively and maliciously hostile to the Spirit of Jesus as each was a kind of distillation of the two worlds from whence they came.

Those present day teachers who place the Sermon on the Mount in some other dispensation than this and so release the Church from its teachings little realize the evil they do. For the Sermon on the Mount gives in brief the characteristics of the Kingdom of renewed men. The blessed poor who mourn for their sins and thirst after righteousness are true sons of the Kingdom. In meekness they show mercy to their enemies; with guileless candor they gaze upon God; surrounded by persecutors they bless and curse not. In modesty they hide their good deeds. They go out of their way to agree with their adversaries and forgive those who sin against them. They serve God in secret in the depth of their hearts and wait with patience for His open reward. They freely surrender their earthly goods rather than use violence to protect them. They lay up their treasures in heaven. They avoid praise and wait for the day of final reckoning to learn who is greatest in the Kingdom of heaven.

If this is a fairly accurate view of things, what can we say then when Christian men vie with one another for place and position? What can we answer when we see them hungrily seeking for praise and honor? How can we excuse that passion for publicity which is so glaringly evident among Christian leaders? What about political ambition in Church circles? What about the fevered palm that is stretched out for more and bigger "love offerings"? What about the shameless egotism among Christians? How can we explain the gross man-worship that habitually blows up one and another popular leader to the size of a colossus? What about the obsequious hand kissing of moneyed men by those purporting to be sound preachers of the gospel?

There is only one answer to these questions; it is simply that in these manifestations we see the world and nothing but the world. No passionate profession of love for "souls" can change evil into good. These are the very sins that crucified Jesus.

It is true also that the grosser manifestations of fallen human nature are part of the kingdom of this world. Organized amusements with their emphasis upon shallow pleasure, the great empires built upon vicious and unnatural habits, unrestrained abuse of the normal appetites, the artificial world called "high society." These all are of the world. They are all part of that which is flesh, which builds upon flesh and must perish with the flesh. And from these things the Christian must flee. All these he must put behind him and in them he must have no part. Against them he must stand quietly but firmly without compromise and without fear.

So whether the world present itself in its uglier aspects or in its subtler and more refined forms, we must recognize it for what it is and repudiate it bluntly. We *must* do this if we would walk with God in our generation as Enoch did in his. A clean break with the world is imperative. "Ye adulterers and adultresses, know ye not that the friendship of the world is enmity with God? whosoever therefore will be a friend of the world is an enemy of God" (James 4:4). "Love not the world, neither the things that are in the world. If any man love the world, the love of the Father is not in him. For all that is in the world, the lust of the flesh, and the lust of the eyes, and the pride of life, is not of the Father, but is of the world" (1 John 2:15-16). These words of God are not before us for our consideration; they are there for our obedience and we have no right to claim the title of Christian unless we follow them.

For myself, I fear any kind of religious stir among Christians that does not lead to repentance and result in a sharp separation of the believer from the world. I am suspicious of any organized revival effort that is forced to play down the hard terms of the Kingdom. No matter how attractive the movement may appear, if it is not founded in righteousness and nurtured in humility it is not of God. If it exploits the flesh it is a religious fraud and should not have the support of any God-fearing Christian. Only that is of God which honors the Spirit and prospers at the expense of the human ego. "That, according as it is written, He that glorieth, let him glory in the Lord."

X

The Spirit-filled Life

BE FILLED WITH THE SPIRIT.
Ephesians 5:18

THAT EVERY CHRISTIAN can be and should be filled
with the Holy Spirit would hardly seem to be a matter for debate among Christians. Yet some will argue
that the Holy Spirit is not for plain Christians but
for ministers and missionaries only. Others hold that
the measure of the Spirit received at regeneration is
identical with that received by the disciples at Pentecost and any hope of additional fullness after conversion simply rests upon error. A few will express
a languid hope that some day they may be filled, and
still others will avoid the subject as one about which
they know very little and which can only cause em-
barrassment.

I want here boldly to assert that it is my happy
belief that every Christian can have a copious out-
pouring of the Holy Spirit in a measure far beyond
that received at conversion, and I might also say, far
beyond that enjoyed by the rank and file of orthodox
believers today. It is important that we get this
straight, for until doubts are removed faith is impossible. God will not surprise a doubting heart with

an effusion of the Holy Spirit, nor will He fill anyone who has doctrinal questions about the possibility of being filled.

To remove doubts and create a confident expectation I recommend a reverent study of the Word of God itself. I am willing to rest my case upon the teachings of the New Testament. If a careful and humble examination of the words of Christ and His apostles does not lead to a belief that we may be filled with the Holy Spirit now, then I see no reason to look elsewhere. For it matters little what this or that religious teacher has said for or against the proposition. If the doctrine is not taught in the Scriptures then it cannot be supported by any argument, and all exhortations to be filled are valueless.

I shall not here present a case for the affirmative. Let the inquirer examine the evidence for himself, and if he decides that there is no warrant in the New Testament for believing that he can be filled with the Spirit, let him shut this book and save himself the trouble of reading further. What I say from here on is addressed to men and women who have gotten over their questions and are confident that when they meet the conditions they may indeed be filled with the Holy Spirit.

Before a man can be filled with the Spirit *he must be sure he wants to be.* And let this be taken seriously. Many Christians want to be filled, but their desire is a vague romantic kind of thing hardly worthy to be called desire. They have almost no knowledge of what it will cost them to realize it.

Let us imagine that we are talking to an inquirer, some eager young Christian, let us say, who has sought us out to learn about the Spirit-filled life. As gently as possible, considering the pointed nature of the questions, we would probe his soul somewhat as follows: "Are you sure you want to be filled with a Spirit who, though He is like Jesus in His gentleness and love, will nevertheless demand to be Lord of your life? Are you willing to let your personality be taken over by another, even if that other be the Spirit of God Himself? If the Spirit takes charge of your life He will expect unquestioning obedience in everything. He will not tolerate in you the self-sins even though they are permitted and excused by most Christians. By the self-sins I mean self-love, self-pity, self-seeking, self-confidence, self-righteousness, self-aggrandizement, self-defense. You will find the Spirit to be in sharp opposition to the easy ways of the world and of the mixed multitude within the precincts of religion. He will be jealous over you for good. He will not allow you to boast or swagger or show off. He will take the direction of your life away from you. He will reserve the right to test you, to discipline you, to chasten you for your soul's sake. He may strip you of many of those borderline pleasures which other Christians enjoy but which are to you a source of refined evil. Through it all He will enfold you in a love so vast, so mighty, so all-embracing, so wondrous that your very losses will seem like gains and your small pains like pleasures. Yet the flesh will whimper under His yoke and cry out against it as a burden too great to bear. And you will be permitted to enjoy the solemn privilege of suffering to 'fill up that which is behind of the afflictions of Christ' in your flesh for His body's sake, which is the Church. Now, with the conditions before you, do you still want to be filled with the Holy Spirit?''

If this appears severe, let us remember that the way of the cross is never easy. The shine and glamour accompanying popular religious movements is as false as the sheen on the wings of the angel of darkness when he for a moment transforms himself into an angel of light. The spiritual timidity that fears to show the cross in its true character is not on any grounds to be excused. It can result only in disappointment and tragedy at last.

Before we can be filled with the Spirit *the desire to be filled must be all-consuming*. It must be for the time the biggest thing in the life, so acute, so intrusive as to crowd out everything else. The degree of fullness in any life accords perfectly with the intensity of true desire. We have as much of God as we actually want. One great hindrance to the Spirit-filled life is the theology of complacency so widely accepted among gospel Christians today. According to this view acute desire is an evidence of unbelief and proof of lack of knowledge of the Scriptures. A sufficient refutation of this position is afforded by the Word of God itself and by the fact that it always fails to produce real saintliness among those who hold it.

Then, I doubt whether anyone ever received that divine afflatus with which we are here concerned who did not first *experience a period of deep anxiety and inward agitation*. Religious contentment is the enemy of the spiritual life always. The biographies of the saints teach that the way to spiritual greatness has always been through much suffering and inward pain. The phrase, "the way of the cross," though it has come in certain circles to denote something very beautiful, even enjoyable, still means to the real Christian what it has always meant, the way of rejection and loss. No one ever enjoyed a cross, just as no one ever enjoyed a gallows.

The Christian who is seeking better things and who has to his consternation found himself in a state of complete self-despair need not be discouraged. Despair with self, where it is accompanied by faith, is a good friend, for it destroys one of the heart's most potent enemies and prepares the soul for the ministration of the Comforter. A sense of utter emptiness, of disappointment and darkness can (if we are alert and wise to what is going on) be the shadow in the valley of shadows that leads on to those fruitful fields that lie further in. If we misunderstand it and resist this visitation of God we may miss entirely every benefit a kind heavenly Father has in mind for us. If we cooperate with God He will take away the natural comforts which have served us as mother and nurse for so long and put us where we can receive no help except from the Comforter Himself. He will tear away that false thing the Chinese call "face" and show us how painfully small we really are. When He is finished with us we will know what our Lord meant when He said, "Blessed are the poor in spirit."

Be sure, however, that in these painful chasten-ings we shall not be deserted by our God. He will never leave us nor forsake us, nor will He be wroth with us nor rebuke us. He will not break His covenant nor alter that which has gone out of His mouth. He will keep us as the apple of His eye and watch over us as a mother watches over her child. His love will not fail even while He is taking us through this experience of self-crucifixion so real, so terrible, that we can express it only by crying, "My God, my God, why hast Thou forsaken me?"

Now let us keep our theology straight about all this. There is not in this painful stripping one remote thought of human merit. The "dark night of the soul" knows not one dim ray of the treacherous light of self-righteousness. We do not by suffering earn the anointing for which we yearn, nor does this devastation of soul make us dear to God nor give us additional favor in His eyes. The value of the stripping experience lies in its power to detach us from life's passing interests and to throw us back upon eternity. It serves to empty our earthly vessels and prepare us for the inpouring of the Holy Spirit.

The filling with the Spirit, then, requires that we give up our all, that we undergo an inward death, that we rid our hearts of that centuries-old accumulation of Adamic trash and open all rooms to the heavenly Guest.

The Holy Spirit is a living Person and should be treated as a person. We must never think of Him as a blind energy nor as an impersonal force. He hears and sees and feels as any person does. He speaks and hears us speak. We can please Him or grieve Him or silence Him as we can any other person. He will respond to our timid effort to know Him and will ever meet us over half the way.

However wonderful the crisis-experience of being filled with the Spirit, we should remember that it is only a means toward something greater: that greater thing is the life-long walk in the Spirit, indwelt, directed, taught and empowered by His mighty Person. And to continue thus to walk in the Spirit requires that we meet certain conditions. These are laid down for us in the sacred Scriptures and are there for all to see.

The Spirit-filled walk demands, for instance, that we live in the Word of God as a fish lives in the sea. By this I do not mean that we study the Bible merely, nor that we take a "course" in Bible doctrine. I mean that we should "meditate day and night" in the sacred Word, that we should love it and feast upon it and digest it every hour of the day and night. When the business of life compels our attention we may yet, by a kind of blessed mental reflex, keep the Word of Truth ever before our minds.

Then if we would please the in-dwelling Spirit we must be all taken up with Christ. The Spirit's present work is to honor Him, and everything He does has this for its ultimate purpose. And we must make our thoughts a clean sanctuary for His holy habitation. He dwells in our thoughts, and soiled thoughts are as repugnant to Him as soiled linen to a king. Above all we must have a cheerful faith that will keep on believing however radical the fluctuation in our emotional states may be.

The Spirit in-dwelt life is not a special de luxe edition of Christianity to be enjoyed by a certain rare and privileged few who happen to be made of finer and more sensitive stuff than the rest. Rather, it is the normal state for every redeemed man and woman the world over. It is "that mystery which hath been hid from ages and from generations, but now is made manifest to his saints: to whom God would make known what is the riches of the glory of this mystery among the gentiles: which is Christ in you, the hope of glory" (Colossians 1:26). Faber, in one of his sweet and reverent hymns, addressed this good word to the Holy Spirit:

> Ocean, wide flowing Ocean, Thou,
>   Of uncreated Love;
> I tremble as within my soul
>   I feel Thy waters move.
>
> Thou art a sea without a shore;
>   Awful, immense Thou art;
> A sea which can contract itself
>   Within my narrow heart.